BENEATH THE VEIL OF THOUGHT

ISBN 978-0-7961-3025-9

First Published in 2024

Beyond The Vale Publishing
www.beyondthevalepublishing.com

BENEATH THE VEIL OF THOUGHT

A JOURNEY TO THE SECRETS OF PERSONAL MASTERY

By

Steyn Rossouw

Table of Contents

The intuitive mind is a sacred gift and the rational mind is a faithful servant. We have created a society that honours the servant and has forgotten the gift.

- Albert Einstein

Foreword

Deep down inside you know you are meant for more.

You know you have untapped potential inside of you.

You need to grow.

You need to think differently.

You need to act differently.

The life you want depends on your thinking and doing.

How?

Change starts with you, but it doesn't start until you do.

> *You are who you are and what you are because of what has gone into your mind. You can change who you are and what you are by changing what goes into your mind.*
>
> - Zig Ziglar

What you need is a road map, an action guide, that teaches you how to change your thinking and your habits so that you can become the person that automatically creates the life you want.

Good news! Steyn Rossouw has written the "how to" action guide that connects your mindset to your actions so that the life you have always dreamed of can become a reality. Beneath the Veil of Thought is your "how to" action guide that will help you unleash the potential trapped inside of you.

Deep, easy to understand and practical.

This is what I love most about this book. The concepts are deep and create lasting change when you apply them to your life. Steyn has presented these concepts in an easy to understand format and then he gives you a practical 30-Day Mind Mastery Challenge that will guide you as you Unleash Your Full Potential.

Go ahead - get started!

Tom Ziglar,

CEO of Zig Ziglar Corporation.

Introduction

In the bustling journey of self-improvement and personal growth, some of us stride resolutely down the path, while others find themselves meandering through the twists and turns. Regardless of our exact position on this transformative road, we all share a common yearning – the pursuit of a better life. Whether it's deeper connections, increased wealth, improved health, or a more fulfilling existence, the desire for advancement resides within each of us. Abraham Maslow encapsulated this aspiration as self-actualization, the pursuit of becoming all that we can be, of embracing our latent potential.

We endeavour to uplift ourselves, to become beacons of the changes we wish to see in the world, recognizing that external manifestations of success are reflections of internal states. Hence, we delve into the troves of self-help literature, practice visualization techniques, recite affirmations, attend seminars, and explore countless other methodologies.

Yet, even as we invest our time and effort, the results often appear fleeting or fall short of our aspirations. The question beckons – why does this cycle persist?

The answer lies in the depths of your consciousness, your hidden reservoir of power. Imagine it as your personal Wizard of Oz, orchestrating events from behind a veil of thoughts, working tirelessly round the clock, unbeknownst to you. This Wizard, your subconscious mind, stands ready to fulfil your wishes, but without a grasp of its operational principles, your desires remain unattainable, like Dorothy stranded in Oz. The key to transforming from captive to commander is understanding.

Let's explore the first revelation: your subconscious mind operates with a simple binary: growth or decay. Like a sophisticated computer program, it processes incoming information without judgment, operating as your habitual patterns dictate – either fostering growth or ushering in decay. As a neural network forms in your brain with each repeated behaviour, the path of least resistance becomes your default route. Changing course is not easy – your subconscious crave the familiar, the comfortable. Therefore, to break the cycle, you must actively choose growth over decay.

Another essential truth: your subconscious mind interprets everything literally. Every thought, every assertion, every self-label is taken as truth and acted upon accordingly. It's akin to having a wish-granting genie – what you say, what you believe, becomes your reality. And while you strive for change, bear in mind that you're seeking growth while your subconscious defaults to the known. Hence, the importance of crafting your desires in a way that eliminates what you don't want, instead of highlighting it.

At the core of transformation lies the power of your beliefs. Your subconscious builds your life based on these beliefs, establishing a cap on your potential. If you think you're limited, your life will reflect that belief. Yet, shifting your beliefs shatters those self-imposed barriers, allowing your life to expand beyond the confines of your previous beliefs.

Change is not easy, for your subconscious operates under the impulse of pleasure-seeking and pain-avoidance. This innate drive, a relic of ancestral survival, resists the unknown and favours the familiar. Overcoming this resistance demands embracing discomfort and forging ahead, for only by persisting can you recalibrate your subconscious mind to accept change.

Remember, your subconscious learns through repetition and emotion. By nourishing new thoughts and behaviours with emotional intensity, you imprint them more deeply, hastening their integration into your being. This phenomenon, where imagination bridges the gap between reality and unreality, empowers you to reshape your reality through vivid visualization.

In this exploration of the human mind's power, we shall journey into the labyrinth of your consciousness. We will unearth the strategies and tools to awaken your inner Wizard, allowing you to command your destiny and sculpt the life you envision. The path is profound, sometimes arduous, but always transformative. As you embark upon this quest, remember, that the power of your thoughts is the rudder steering your ship through the vast sea of possibilities.

Personal Mastery and Organizational Learning

In the landscape of our ever-disruptive era, the concept of personal mastery takes on a profound role within the realm of organizational learning. In this dynamic environment, the ability of an organization to learn and adapt has become its sole enduring advantage. As Peter Senge aptly recognized, the link between personal mastery and organizational learning is inseparable: "Organizations learn only through individuals who learn. Individual learning does not guarantee organizational learning. But without it, no organizational learning occurs." The synergy between individual growth and the collective evolution of an organization is the catalyst that propels progress.

The journey towards personal mastery, however, is not devoid of challenges. These constraints and trials, starkly highlighted by the current reality, are what mould our capacity to navigate the creative tension that lies between our present state and our envisioned future. In this liminal space, mastery finds its form – an artful dance between where we stand and where we aspire to be, what we are and what God has created us to be.

> *Man was designed for accomplishment, engineered for success and endowed with the seeds of greatness*
>
> *– Zig Ziglar.*

Values: A Guiding Compass

In the voyage towards mastery, values emerge as the compass that guides our course. Stephen Covey's metaphor of the compass eloquently captures the essence of how values steer us towards our vision. When we possess a clear understanding of our personal values, and by extension, the values that underpin the organizations we lead or contribute to, we are endowed with a powerful decision-making tool, especially when faced with uncertainty.

The voyage of personal mastery also poses an intriguing question: When we align ourselves with certain values, how willing are we to uphold those values in the face of sacrifice?

To illustrate, consider the Titanic's tragic tale. The decisions made during that fateful journey, driven by the values of aesthetics over safety, expose the complex interplay of values and decisions. Likewise, in our own lives, we encounter choices that might not be life-threatening but carry potential career implications. The clash between the value of integrity and the value of self-preservation is a prime example of the challenges we face on the path of personal mastery. I believe it is only in the relentless pursuit of honesty that we are afforded the privilege of integrity. In this pursuit self-preservation can easily clash with our pursuit.

Living in alignment with our values is a formidable feat, as demonstrated by these real-world scenarios. Addressing these challenges requires a conscious exploration of our values and a deliberate practice of integrating them into our decision-making processes and integrating them into our daily habits.

Perspective: The Multifaceted Lens

We see things not as they are but as how we perceive, believe and expect them to be. All of our reality lies in our perception.

Central to the journey of personal mastery is the cultivation of perspective. This encompasses understanding our mental models, recognizing the context, culture, and relationships that surround us, and expanding our outlook beyond our immediate mindset. Imagine the game of football as a metaphor for perspective:

As a player, your focus centres on the ball and the other players.

As a spectator, your attention shifts to both individual plays and the team's performance against the opposition.

A commentator perceives the game's impact on the league table.

An academic delves into the game's historical, social, and symbolic dimensions.

An extra-terrestrial observer would question the game's purpose and relevance.

In life, we often function as players engrossed in the pursuit of immediate goals, seldom considering the broader picture. To attain personal mastery, we must transcend this limited view, adopting the perspectives of both the spectator and the commentator. By doing so, we gain the ability to step back from our own mental constructs, critically assess situations in relation to our vision and values and develop a holistic comprehension of the world around us.

In essence, personal mastery involves a harmonious convergence of individual growth, organizational learning, value alignment, and expanded perspective. This journey is not one of convenience or ease, but rather an intentional commitment to continuous growth, self-awareness, and a profound grasp of the interconnectedness of our inner world and the external reality. As we tread this path, we step into the realm of true mastery, where our actions, choices, and contributions become a symphony that shapes not only our lives but the trajectory of the organizations and communities we touch.

Many of us lead our lives without giving much consideration to our inner thought processes. We fail to pay attention to how our mind works, what it fears, what it pays attention to, the story it tells itself and what it chooses to ignore. We often neglect one of the most crucial and influential aspects of our lives.

THE POWER OF OUR THOUGHTS

A New Life Through Mind Mastery

In the intricate tapestry of transformation, a new life finds its genesis within a new mind. To embark on a journey of change, one must reconfigure the manner in which the mind operates. A pivotal truth emerges: the simultaneous existence of negative and positive thoughts is a paradox. One will always supersede the other, and the choice rests upon us. Just as we are creatures of habit, so too are our minds. It is imperative that we cultivate a landscape where empowering thoughts and positive emotions reign supreme.

To effect change in the external realm, an internal revolution is paramount. This crucial step is often overlooked. Many endeavour to alter their surroundings directly, but lasting transformation remains elusive without a concurrent metamorphosis in thoughts and beliefs. The conscious mind emerges as a canvas on which success, happiness, health, and prosperity must be vividly painted. Just as weeds are plucked to ensure the growth of desired plants, the negativity of fear and worry must be uprooted from the garden of the mind. Occupy your conscious mind with the anticipation of the best outcomes, and diligently curate thoughts aligned with your aspirations.

Yet, it is vital to acknowledge that mastery over the mind transcends the realm of philosophy; it is a living, breathing practice woven into the fabric of daily life. Mind mastery does not equate to mere positive thinking; it is a discipline that delves deeper. Positive thinking, while enhancing performance, lacks permanence. It is a stepping stone, not the final destination. To wield mastery over the mind demands a systematic approach, a ritual of daily practices diligently repeated until they crystallize into habit.

No longer confined to motivational rhetoric, mind mastery is now a realm of structured action. It involves a sequence of daily rituals, meticulously performed, sculpting an unbreakable habit. The fallacy of fleeting motivation is replaced by the potency of consistent practice. Mind mastery fashions a mental infrastructure where positivity, focus, and growth become the pillars that shape every action, reaction, and decision.

The theme of this transformative symphony underscores the synergy between internal and external metamorphosis. It echoes the timeless wisdom that true change initiates within before it manifests without. A new life blossoms from the seeds of a new mindset, rooted in mindful choices and deliberate actions. As the daily rhythm of mind mastery reverberates through your existence, you become the conductor orchestrating the symphony of your life. The melody of empowerment and success becomes your anthem, and the pursuit of mastery is a constant cadence in your journey of evolution.

In the intricate realm of human biology, the brain stands as an awe-inspiring masterpiece. Capable of an astonishing 38 trillion operations per second, it operates at a pace 500 times faster than even the most advanced supercomputers on Earth. This neural powerhouse, comprising a mere 2% of our body's weight, commands a remarkable 20% of the body's energy and oxygen consumption. This juxtaposition of size and demand underscores its paramount significance in shaping our existence.

Within the convolutions of the brain lie 86 billion brain cells, each a testament to the complexity of our cognitive machinery. This intricate web of cells generates a subtle 12-25 watts of electricity, a testament to its incredible efficiency. Information within this neural matrix travels at speeds of up to 268 miles per hour, a testament to the swift and intricate exchanges that underlie our thoughts, emotions, and perceptions.

Yet, beneath the surface, an enigmatic truth surfaces – the conscious realm of our lives holds less sway than we assume. An astonishing 95% of our decisions, the bedrock of our daily choices, occur in the recesses of the subconscious mind. This revelation challenges the notion of complete conscious control, highlighting the profound interplay between the conscious and the hidden.

A tapestry of thought weaves itself within our minds each day, yielding an average of around 50,000 thoughts. Yet, an unsettling 70% of these thoughts tilt towards negativity, a statistic that illuminates the inherent human struggle with self-doubt and apprehension.

But amid this complex interplay of cognitive mechanics, emerges a beacon of hope, Mind Mastery. This practice offers a transformative tool to reshape our mental landscape, empowering us to transcend the shackles of negative thought patterns. Mind Mastery paves the way towards a more positive and fulfilling life, as we learn to steer our thoughts, align our focus, and cultivate an environment of growth and optimism.

In the symphony of existence, the brain stands as the conductor, orchestrating the harmony of thoughts, emotions, and actions. Mind Mastery emerges as the score, guiding us towards a harmonious melody of empowerment. It is the journey of taking command over our mental realm, a journey that unveils the ability to rewrite the narrative of our lives.

As we journey through Mind Mastery, we take a conscious step towards reclaiming our agency, sculpting a reality that resonates with positivity and fulfilment. Each positive thought, each intentional shift, and every instance of choosing empowerment becomes a brushstroke in the masterpiece of our lives. By wielding the power of our mind, we shape our destiny and embrace the promise of a life imbued with purpose, joy, and resilience.

You have to train your mind to be stronger than your emotions or else you will lose yourself every time.

- Steyn Rossouw

Personal Mastery: The Unending Journey of Growth

In the realm of wisdom, an old Chinese proverb whispers a profound truth: "If you read a book a thousand times, you are bound to understand it." This adage resonates with the concept of personal mastery, a path many seek, whether consciously or not. Personal mastery encapsulates the essence of ceaseless improvement and the art of perceiving life through a transformed lens.

In my perception, mastery is not an elusive destination, but rather, a dynamic mindset. The crux of mastering anything lies in the unwavering belief that our abilities are boundlessly improvable. It calls for unwavering dedication, consistent effort, and a deliberate practice that weaves into our daily lives.

Mastery thrives on an unyielding commitment to constant growth. It commences with the understanding that complete mastery is an asymptote, a goal perpetually approached but never fully attained. Therein lies its beauty and paradox a never-ending journey of improvement. This perspective propels us to continually surpass our former selves, always striving to elevate our standards.

In essence, mastery is an ongoing quest, where the delight dwells in the pursuit rather than the destination. The allure lies in the eternal dance of reaching but never touching the final pinnacle of perfection. It is this very enigma that drives top performers, propelling them to refine their skills, continuously innovate, and forever learn. Their ardour to be better every day, irrespective of their proficiency, embodies the essence of mastery.

Jeff Bezos, the visionary behind Amazon, underscores this philosophy in his 'Day 1' principle. This philosophy asserts that regardless of past triumphs, success should not breed complacency. The same vigour, curiosity, and agility that are kindled on day one must be carried forward, propelling growth even in the face of achievement.

Yet, the shadow of 'Day 2' looms—the antithesis of mastery, characterized by stasis, decline, and ultimately, extinction. When we succumb to comfort, resist change, and relinquish the pursuit of improvement, 'Day 2' casts its pall. Bezos' warning becomes an echoing reminder that the journey of mastery is a deliberate and intentional, lifelong choice.

To embark on the path of mastery, we must foster a growth mindset, a tenacious pursuit of learning, and an unyielding drive to progress. Amid the journey, we may encounter discomfort as we shatter boundaries and challenge our limitations, but within this challenge lies the opportunity to cultivate grit, a trait that can be honed and strengthened like a muscle.

Personal mastery transcends its definition, it becomes a beacon guiding our effective existence and successful career. Now more than ever, this truth stands unshaken in the currents of history.

So, what does personal mastery entail? It is the art of intentional living, a purposeful journey toward a vision rooted in alignment with our values. In this odyssey, we engage in constant self-discovery, learning about both ourselves and the world that envelops us.

The power of personal mastery lies in its congruence with self-leadership. Both domains demand self-awareness, self-management, and an insatiable quest for self-improvement.

"Know thyself", an age-old adage etched into the Temple of Apollo, serves as the compass to navigate this era of AI and social media.

Personal mastery is not a solitary endeavour; it ripples into the capacity to lead others. Effective leadership starts with mastering oneself before influencing others. The current landscape yearns for accountable individuals who proactively take ownership. The mantra "Nothing starts unless you start", becomes our anthem, propelling us forward regardless of our starting point.

The journey of personal mastery isn't a simple one, it's an exploration into the uncharted territories of our identity, values, and visions. It's a commitment to authenticity in an era where algorithms seek to shape our identities. To be genuine and confident, we must first ascertain our essence.

Your journey to personal mastery is a profound voyage, one that unveils both your strengths and areas for growth. It beckons you to become an author of your narrative, to embrace the uncertainty and richness of life. Personal mastery is the art of growth, an unending journey from survival to success, from success to significance, and from significance to legacy. In this grand voyage, remember that the elevator to success is out of service, you'll have to climb the stairs, one step at a time.

The Power of Being, Doing, and Giving: Crafting a Legacy of Purpose

Zig Ziglar's wisdom resonates through the ages, reminding us that life's journey follows a profound rhythm: "You have to be before you can do, you have to do before you can have, and you have to have before you can give". These words echo with the essence of purpose, shaping a legacy that transcends time. But what do they truly entail?

At their core, these words speak of alignment aligning who we are with what we do, allowing us to amass the treasures of life so we can then share abundantly. This journey is underpinned by an unbreakable truth: You cannot give what you don't possess. To empower others to reach their potential, we must first tap into our own, extending a hand only when we're firmly rooted.

The secret lies in becoming the right kind of person who engages in the right kind of actions. By nurturing our being, by embodying values, principles, and virtues, we cultivate a fertile ground from which transformative actions can sprout. These actions pave the path to our desired possessions, material and immaterial, tangible and intangible.

> *What you get by achieving your goals is not nearly as important as who you become by reaching your goals*
>
> – Joe Sabah.

It's the fulfilment of a universal equation, effort, intention, and persistence that yield the rewards.

As we accumulate, we recognize the power to give expands exponentially, but this giving is not mere charity; it's the potent alchemy of sharing what we've earned through dedication, grit, and perseverance. When we bestow upon others the tools to reach new heights, we forge a legacy that extends beyond ourselves; a legacy rooted in creating ripples of empowerment, fostering growth, and shaping brighter futures.

Our journey commences with a profound inquiry into the "Why" that reverberates within. The questions of why I exist, and why I do what I do, fuels the quest for purpose. The echoes of the past resonate, where ancient Greeks etched "Know Thyself" upon their temples, an invitation to introspect, to unearth the motivations and intentions that guide our actions.

This pursuit of self-knowledge, a cross-cultural endeavour, unveils the core of religions, philosophies, and personal development. Yet, the very brilliance that enables our minds to question all also leads us to question ourselves. The perennial inquiries "Who am I? Can I change?" pervades our consciousness.

In this exploration, psychology has uncovered a striking revelation, the profound impact of self-belief on our behaviours and achievements. Those who believe in their intelligence perform better in tests, not because they are inherently smarter, but due to their unwavering belief. The power of beliefs extends to physical feats; the placebo effect demonstrates how a mere belief in an energy drink boosts physical performance.

Our beliefs are transformative forces.

Harnessing this power entails training our minds, cultivating awareness, and harnessing the influence of beliefs to our advantage. This is a journey of introspection, a voyage into the core of self. It's about recognizing the beliefs that propel us forward and the ones that hold us back dismantling the latter and empowering the former.

To embark on this journey, clarity becomes our guiding light. Just as one reads the introduction before delving into a book, we must comprehend our starting point. We often find ourselves content as walking generalities, traversing the days with no clear direction. The transition from survival to success demands clarity, a clear destination and a mapped route.

The journey begins with setting intentions. What do we aspire to be? What do we desire to have? What actions are congruent with our essence? What will we leave behind as our legacy? Life's purpose flourishes when we actively engage in growth. With each choice, we inch closer to growth or drift towards decline. The power lies in the clarity of our intentions.

In the grand symphony of existence, our purpose comes alive when we nurture a growth mindset, cultivate clarity, and engage in intentional actions. As the chapters of our lives unfold, let us remember that mastery thrives in perpetual motion, between being and doing, between giving and receiving, crafting a legacy that etches its mark on hearts, transcending lifetimes. For in this world, we are either growing or fading, and our purpose ignites when we choose the former over the latter.

About the Author

Steyn Rossouw is a renowned expert in the fields of personal growth, mind power and sales. With a diverse background that includes eight years in the armed forces as a specialist combat operator, Steyn embarked on a new career path in business and professional selling. However, his initial foray into sales proved challenging, with no sales made despite his relentless efforts.

Determined to turn his situation around, Steyn immersed himself in the teachings of sales luminaries Zig Ziglar and Tom Hopkins. This pivotal moment marked a profound shift in his life, propelling him to become a top salesman and eventually a top sales manager. His exceptional performance earned him the esteemed title of Top International Sales Manager of the Year.

In 1993, Steyn attended the Mind Power Training by John Kehoe, which further deepened his understanding of the vast potential of the human mind. Intrigued by the transformative techniques taught by Kehoe, Steyn realized there was much more to the human mind than society commonly acknowledged. Fuelling his curiosity, he sought to gain a higher level of understanding, leading him to train under the world-renowned Sir Andrew Newton as a hypnotherapist. This exploration into the realms of the conscious and subconscious mind allowed Steyn to uncover powerful insights into sales, personal growth, and success.

Drawing upon the collective wisdom of Zig Ziglar, Tom Hopkins,

John Kehoe, and Sir Andrew Newton, Steyn recognized a common denominator that underpinned success in both personal and business realms—the control of the human mind. Guided by his deep fascination with human behaviour and mind power, Steyn has spent the past 30 years building businesses, training and mentoring thousands of individuals in entrepreneurship, leadership, sales success, motivation, personal mastery, and mind power.

Steyn's philosophy is rooted in the belief that knowledge is only truly powerful when applied. He firmly advocates for continual self-improvement, regardless of one's stage in life. Whether the goal is developing a better mindset or increasing profits, Steyn emphasizes the importance of progress and moving forward. His unwavering belief is that the only limits that exist are the ones we impose upon ourselves.

If you are seeking life-changing courses and profound insights from Steyn Rossouw, please visit his website for more information and to embark on your own transformative journey.

www.steynrossouw.com

May you only find blessings in this book.

Steyn Rossouw

Chapter 1: The Journey of Transformation: From Survival to Legacy

You don't have to be great to start, but you have to start to be great!

- Zig Ziglar –

The journey of transformation is a profound odyssey that takes you from the realm of survival to the pinnacle of legacy. It's a journey of self-discovery, growth, and empowerment that holds the power to reshape your entire existence. As we embark on this transformative quest, we'll delve into the fundamental principles that guide our path and illuminate the way forward.

Starting with Purpose: Discovering Your "Why"

Meet Emily, a determined young woman who overcame adversity with the power of her "why". Emily grew up in a modest family, facing financial struggles and limited opportunities. Despite the challenges, she held onto a dream, to become a doctor and make a difference in her community. Her "why" was rooted in her desire to provide better healthcare for her family and others who lacked access to medical services.

Driven by her "why", Emily pursued her education relentlessly. She studied late into the night, worked multiple jobs to fund her education, and persevered through setbacks. Her unwavering dedication was fuelled by the profound impact she envisioned making in the lives of others. Her "why" was not just a dream; it was a lifeline that pulled her forward when the journey got tough.

Every journey begins with a single step, and the first step on the path of transformation is discovering your "why". Your "why" is your purpose, your driving force, the deep-rooted reason that fuels your desire for change. It's the spark that ignites the fire within you and propels you forward, even in the face of challenges.

Why is having a big "why" important? Your "why" provides you with clarity and direction. It's the compass that keeps you on course when the waters get rough. When you know why you're pursuing transformation, every obstacle becomes a stepping stone, and every setback becomes a setup for a comeback.

Unlocking Your Gifts, Skills, and Talents

As you set out on your journey, remember that you possess unique gifts, skills, and talents that are waiting to be unleashed. These are the tools that will propel you toward your goals and dreams. Just as a sculptor uses their tools to shape a masterpiece, you too can harness your innate abilities to craft a life of fulfilment and purpose.

Your gifts are the essence of who you are, and your skills are the keys that unlock your potential. Embrace your talents and nurture them with passion and dedication. They hold the key to unlocking doors of opportunity and creating a life that aligns with your true self.

The Trifecta of Transformation: Mindset, Strategy, Action

In the realm of transformation, success is not merely about chance, it's about intentionality. It's about cultivating the right habits that foster growth and progress. The trifecta of transformation consists of three crucial elements: mindset, strategy, and action.

Mindset: The habit of right thinking is the cornerstone of transformation. Your thoughts shape your reality, and by adopting a positive and empowered mindset, you can overcome self-doubt, fears, and limitations. A growth-oriented mindset is the fertile ground from which your journey sprouts.

Carefully watch your thoughts, for they become your words. Manage and watch your words, for they will become your actions. Consider and judge your actions, for they have become your habits. Acknowledge and watch your habits, for they shall become your values

-Gandhi

Strategy: The habit of right planning is the blueprint for your transformation. Without a plan, your "why" remains a distant dream. Develop a strategy that outlines your goals, the steps you need to take, and the milestones you'll achieve along the way. A well-crafted strategy guides your actions and keeps you accountable. The great Zig Ziglar said, "When you develop a game plan to get what you want, you develop a belief that you can get it."

Action: The habit of right implementation turns intentions into reality. It's not enough to think and plan, you must take action. Embrace the discomfort of stepping out of your comfort zone. Every action you take brings you one step closer to your goals. You see in life, lots of people know what to do, but very few people actually do what they know. Knowing is not enough. "You must take action. The path to success is to take massive determined action." – Tony Robbins.

The Be-Do-Have Principle: Crafting Your Journey

The Be-Do-Have principle, coined by the legendary Zig Ziglar, encapsulates the essence of the transformation journey. It's the pathway that leads from survival to legacy, from existence to significance.

Survival: You find yourself in survival mode until you decide who you want to be and put a plan in place to become that person. Survival is the starting point, a call to awaken your inner potential.

Stability: As you embark on the journey of transformation, you transition from survival to stability. Stability is the realm where you move beyond survival mode by preparing and doing what's necessary to become the person you aspire to be.

Success: The journey from stability to success is marked by diligent effort and dedication. You achieve success when you embody the person you've strived to become and reap the rewards of your transformational journey. Success is the result of perfection, hard work, learning from failure, loyalty, and persistence. My mentor, Zig Ziglar, said, "Success occurs when opportunity meets preparation." It is imperative to understand what success is and what it isn't. One thing is for sure; success is not measured in money. Success means doing the best we can with what we have. Success is the doing, not the getting; in the trying, not the triumph. Success is a personal standard, reaching for the highest that is in us, becoming all that God created us to be.

Significance: The transition from success to significance is a transformational leap. It's the stage where your focus shifts from personal success to uplifting others. By helping your customers become who they want to be, you step into a realm of profound impact and significance.

Legacy: The pinnacle of the journey is legacy, a testament to a life lived with purpose and intention. Legacy is forged when you empower others to be, do, and have more than they thought possible. It's a gift that reverberates through time, shaping the world for generations to come.

Legacy as a Reflection of Giving Without Expectation

Legacy goes beyond inheritance, it's what you leave in people. Your legacy is a testament to your life's impact, values, and inspiration. The journey from survival to legacy involves embodying the principles of becoming, doing, having, and giving.

Giving Without Expectation: As you give without expecting anything in return, you contribute to a world of abundance. This principle embodies the essence of legacy, extending kindness, support, and resources without strings attached. By enriching others, you become part of a collective tapestry of growth.

Embracing the Power of Kindness: The Zig It Experience

In the year 2017, I embarked on a transformative journey that was deeply influenced by the teachings of the Ziglar family. Their philosophy of "random acts of kindness" echoed the life's work of the renowned Zig Ziglar himself. Little did I know that this philosophy would soon shape a profound experience during my trip to Los Angeles.

After immersing myself in the wisdom of the Ziglar family at their headquarters in Dallas, Texas, my wife and I decided to extend our journey with a few days in Los Angeles. Our destination was the Hilton Hotel near Universal Studios. Excitement filled the air as we arrived, only to realize that we had arrived well before the designated check-in time.

Drawing from the belief that kindness is a universal language and that everything unfolds as it should, I decided to take action. I approached the booking desk with hope in my heart, armed with the idea of "Zigging it." My wife, intrigued by my confidence, questioned how I intended to secure a room so early. With a smile, I responded that I would put the power of kindness to the test. Everything is energy and vibration everything is connected and what you sow you will reap.

At the initial attempt, our eagerness was met with the truth, we were indeed early, and our room was not yet ready. Undeterred, I took a moment to enjoy a cup of coffee, embracing the idea that everything unfolds in its own time. After a brief interlude, I returned to the booking desk, much to my wife's amusement. Once again, I was informed that our room wasn't available due to the four-hour gap.

But then, as if guided by an invisible hand, the lady behind the desk uttered the words that astounded me. Without any prompting from me, she said, "Let me see what I can do for you, Mr. Rossouw." Before I could react, she smiled and exclaimed, "Well, what do you know? We have a room ready for you. I hope you'll enjoy it."

Grateful and amazed, I expressed my appreciation to her and assured her that a standard room would suffice. However, my wife and I were in for an astonishing surprise. As we entered the room, we were met with the reality that she had granted us a suite, without charging any extra fees. At that moment, the impact of kindness hit me in a profound way.

This experience ignited a spark within me, leading to the creation of the "Zig It" card game, a game designed to pay forward acts of kindness each day. The lesson was clear: we often overlook the simple truth that what we put into the universe echoes back to us in ways we can't always predict. We tend to forget that we all have a fundamental purpose, the purpose of making a difference for at least one person a day, to spread kindness, hope and encouragement.

In a world where we sometimes forget the importance of giving, my encounter with the power of kindness reinforced that our actions can create ripples of positivity. The philosophy of "Zigging it" became more than just a saying; it became a reminder that even the smallest acts of kindness can yield unexpected rewards.

As we journey through life, let us remember that the universe responds to the energy we put out into the world. By embracing the philosophy of "Zigging it," we open ourselves to the infinite possibilities that emerge when we give without expectation. In giving, we not only touch the lives of others but also cultivate a legacy of compassion, generosity, and meaningful connections.

As you embark on your journey from survival to legacy, remember that your "why" is the guiding star that lights your way. Just as Emily's "why" propelled her to overcome challenges, your purpose can empower you to become the person you aspire to be. With each step, you'll embrace the principles of becoming, doing, having, and giving, a symphony that leads to a life of abundance, impact, and enduring legacy.

Remember that you have the power to sculpt your destiny. The journey from survival to legacy is a testament to your resilience, your courage, and your unwavering commitment to growth. It's a journey that unfolds one step at a time, and with each step, you draw closer to realizing your full potential and leaving a lasting imprint on the world. Each day becoming more of your true self, each day becoming a better version of yourself. Each day becoming all that God created you to be.

Chapter 2: It Starts with Your Mind

You are where you are and what you are as a result of what has gone into your mind. You can change where you are and what you are by changing what goes into your mind.

- Zig Ziglar

The foundation of personal mastery, the cornerstone upon which a life of purpose and fulfilment is built, lies within the realm of your own mind. Zig Ziglar's words encapsulate a profound truth, one that invites us to grasp the reins of our own destiny and to acknowledge the role our minds play in shaping the quality of our lives.

This power hinges on what psychologists refer to as an "internal locus of control." This perspective embodies a deep awareness of our responsibility for the trajectory of our lives and the achievements we carve out. While it might be easy to point fingers, to assign blame to others or circumstances, to construct elaborate excuses for perceived shortcomings, it's these very excuses that trap us in a cycle of stagnation.

The real world is a tapestry of stories, stories of individuals who emerged from the depths of adversity, who overcame colossal obstacles, and who defied odds that seemed insurmountable. They weren't always born into privilege; they weren't always dealt a winning hand. Yet, what set them apart was their refusal to bow to excuses, their decision to rise, and their commitment to growth.

Making excuses might offer temporary solace, but it rarely advances us. The reality is that individuals have climbed out of chasms far deeper than the ones we find ourselves in today. The question isn't whether life is fair or whether challenges exist— the question is how we respond to these challenges.

Responsibility, in its truest form, is recognizing our power to respond to circumstances. It's acknowledging that while certain events might not be our fault, they are certainly our responsibility to address. When this shift occurs, transformation unfolds. The very fabric of our existence alters when we cease to be victims of circumstance and step into the role of active creators of our reality.

In essence, taking responsibility is becoming "response-able". It's embracing the ability to craft a deliberate response rather than reacting impulsively. Reacting is a knee-jerk reflex, an autopilot mode triggered by instinct. Responding, on the other hand, emanates from a place of contemplation, an acknowledgement that every choice we make carries weight.

Consider your brain, the remarkable organ that orchestrates your thoughts, emotions, and actions. It was created to ensure survival, not happiness. It's up to you to bridge the gap between survival and fulfilment, to harness your cognitive faculties for the purpose of thriving. Happiness isn't bestowed upon you, it's cultivated by you.

As you journey through life, remember that happiness, success, and fulfilment are the by-products of conscious choices. It's the result of recognizing that while you can't control everything that happens, you can control how you respond to everything that happens to you. Your mind is your most powerful tool, a chisel that shapes the sculpture of your life. So, take the reins, mould your reality, and embrace the journey of mastering your mind, a journey that unfolds as you embrace the power of choice and the responsibility that accompanies it.

We are ultimately the sum total of the choices we make, as my mentor and friend Tom Ziglar often points out it is sometimes a very simple question "is what you are doing taking you closer to your goal or further away?"

Life does not happen to you, but life happens for you.

- Tony Robbins

Chapter 3: The Power of Your Mind

You are who you are and what you are because of what has gone into your mind. You can change who you are and what you are by changing what goes into your mind.

- Zig Ziglar

"So, what is the all-important ingredient? The all-important ingredient is you. Nothing starts unless you do."

Indeed, you are the key to unlocking your potential, the catalyst for change, and the master of your destiny. Yet, it's not just your physical presence, it's the realm of your mind where your journey begins and thrives. Your thoughts, beliefs, focus, and emotions, all stem from the epicentre of your mind.

Each individual carries a unique narrative, and the most pivotal tale is the one you narrate to yourself daily. Furthermore, where your mind leads, your body follows suit.

Consider energy levels, for instance. When you're feeling drained and fatigued, your inclination might be to modify your diet or exercise routine. Yet, more often than not, it's the state of your mind that requires attention first.

The journey from thought to action is the cornerstone of creation. Every aspect of existence, whether relationships, careers, or finances, hinges on this fundamental principle. Imagine wanting to pursue your dream job while remaining chained to your current employment. Envision striving to mend a broken financial situation while deeply entrenched in debt.

Change must begin somewhere, and that starting point is within you. It takes root within your mind, within your thoughts and convictions.

The process of transformation adheres to a universal rule: "First comes the thought, then comes the action." Everything you experience, every step you take, originates as a thought. The trajectory of your life hinges on these initial seeds of cognition. Yet, many fail to recognize this pivotal juncture, allowing thoughts to flutter by unnoticed and unanalysed.

Your life's landscape is interconnected, rife with dependencies and complexities. But at the core, change starts as a spark within your mind, a conscious decision to shift, improve, and grow. Your career, your relationships, and indeed, your entire existence all bloom from the fertile soil of your thoughts.

Picture your mind as a garden, an expanse of fertile soil awaiting cultivation. Plant the seeds of positivity, nurture and nourish them with intention, water them with your focus, and regularly weed out negativity. This metaphor encapsulates the profound truth that your reality is a reflection of your thoughts and what you choose to nurture.

In this garden of the mind, you have the power to shape your own destiny. The grass is not necessarily greener on the other side, it's greener where you water it, where you invest your care, attention, and effort. It's a testament to the idea that your thoughts, like seeds, bear the potential to flourish into a lush landscape of possibilities.

Your mind is your realm of creation. This is the place where only you have control. Harness its power to cultivate your aspirations, foster change, and mould your life in the image you envision. You are the gardener of your mind's landscape, and by tending to your thoughts and beliefs, you cultivate the very essence of your being.

Chapter 4: The Symbiotic Dance of the Inner and Outer Worlds

Whatever results you're getting, be they rich or poor, good or bad, positive or negative, always remember that your outer world is simply a reflection of your inner world. If things aren't going well in your outer life, it's because things aren't going well in your inner life. It's that simple.

- T. Harv Eker

We live in two worlds simultaneously. It's akin to being the intermediary in an ongoing conversation between two dear friends. One of these friends resides within you, within the confines of your thoughts, emotions, and dreams. This inner world is a place where your happiness, self-confidence, and even your fears find their home. It's a realm that you craft, shaped by the stories you tell yourself and the beliefs you hold close to your heart.

The other friend, on the other hand, exists beyond your physical self. This is the external world, the stage upon which the grand theatre of life unfolds. It's a world brimming with circumstances, situations, and interactions, all of which construct your tangible reality. While you may not have complete dominion over every facet of this outer world, you undeniably possess the power to mould your responses and actions within it.

Now, consider this possibility: What if you could emancipate yourself from the ceaseless cycle of mere reaction? Instead of being at the mercy of external events, what if you could consciously choose how to respond? What if your thoughts and actions could align harmoniously with your innermost desires and values?

Here lies the profound revelation: Your inner world and outer world are not inextricably bound. Your inner realm need not be a mere reflection of the outer; it can be a wellspring of creativity, a place where new realities are born.

Envision your inner world as a mirror, reflecting your reactions to the stimuli of the outer world. Mastering this mirror transforms you from a passive observer into an active creator of your emotional landscape. You become the artist wielding the brush, painting the canvas of your own feelings.

Now, imagine leveraging the power of your inner realm to catalyse changes in the outer world. Instead of being passive, you become a proactive force, shaping the course of your life. You transition from reacting to creating, from coping to thriving.

This shift, from passive reaction to purposeful creation, is where your true power resides. It unveils a realm of infinite possibilities that await your exploration. Your inner and outer worlds can collaborate, with your inner world nurturing your growth and your outer world becoming the canvas upon which you paint your aspirations.

As you embark on the journey of navigating these two worlds, you are on a path of profound self-discovery and empowerment. You can mould your inner world, and in doing so, you possess the ability to transform your outer reality. It's a transformative journey that unlocks your potential and allows you to shape your life in alignment with your deepest desires.

Chapter 5: The Tale of Two Wolves

Strength is forged in the fires of determination.

- Steyn Rossouw

This brings to mind the timeless parable of the two wolves. A tale that encapsulates the eternal struggle between positive and negative influences within our minds.

An old Cherokee legend tells of a grandfather imparting wisdom to his grandson. He shares a metaphor that encapsulates the battle of thoughts that rages within each of us, a struggle between two wolves.

The first wolf embodies negativity. It symbolizes fear, anger, envy, self-doubt and resentment. It thrives on the energy of doubt, pessimism and self-sabotage. This wolf's presence leads to stagnation, misery and a life mired in darkness.

The second wolf, in stark contrast, personifies positivity. It represents love, kindness, courage, confidence, and compassion. It thrives on hope, optimism, and empowerment. This wolf's energy fuels growth, fulfilment, and a life illuminated by the light of possibilities.

The young boy, curious and contemplative, asks his grandfather, "Which wolf wins?"

The wise elder, with a knowing smile, replies, "The one you feed."

This allegory speaks to the essence of personal mastery, the power to choose, to direct the focus of your mind, and to cultivate the thoughts that serve your growth and purpose. It underscores the fact that the battles of life are first fought in the arena of the mind.

In the journey toward personal mastery, the wolves are not external forces, but the facets of your own mind. You possess the ability to decide which wolf you nourish, which thoughts you empower, and ultimately, which wolf prevails.

Just as a garden requires consistent care and attention, so does your mind. Your daily choices, your daily habits, your beliefs, and the stories you tell yourself shape your reality. When you choose to feed the wolf of positivity, you fuel your aspirations and create an environment conducive to growth and success.

This allegory underscores the pivotal role your mind plays in your journey toward personal mastery. It reinforces the notion that, by feeding the wolf of positivity through conscious thought, you set in motion a series of actions that shape your destiny.

Remember that your mind is a garden, and your thoughts are the seeds. Nourish the seeds of empowerment, optimism, and resilience, and you will witness the transformation of your inner landscape. Embrace this tale of two wolves as a reminder that the power to shape your reality lies within you.

In the next chapter, we delve deeper into the intricacies of thought patterns and how they shape our perceptions and actions on a daily basis.

Chapter 6: The Dance of Cause and Effect

Thoughts become things through the principle of cause and effect. When you think certain thoughts repeatedly, you are planting a seed in the spiritual world that will bloom in the physical world.

- Catherine Wishart

In the grand story of life, there's a fundamental truth that echoes through time: everything follows a set of rules, and everything has a reason behind it. This fundamental idea shapes the very core of our existence. As we explore Chapter 6, we uncover the profound implications of this principle, revealing the threads that weave our destinies.

Universal Laws Affect Everyone:

Picture the universe as a complex web of laws, guiding every atom, thought, and action in an intricate dance. Just like the way planets follow the laws of gravity, we, too, are bound by these universal laws. These laws steer the ebb and flow of our lives.

Understanding the Law of Cause and Effect:

The Law of Cause and Effect is like a universal law that says for every action, there's a reaction or consequence. It reminds us that nothing happens by pure chance or accident; there's always a reason behind every outcome. This law teaches us that we're not passive spectators in our lives but active creators who can influence our experiences through our choices and actions.

This law isn't limited to individuals; it operates on a larger scale too. It shows us that our thoughts, words, and actions send out ripples that come back to us in various ways. It teaches us to be mindful of what we put into the world because it has the power to shape our reality and affect others.

The Responsibility Principle:

The Law of Cause and Effect is built on the principle of responsibility. It calls us to take ownership of our thoughts, emotions, choices, and actions. This principle acknowledges that we are the architects of our reality and that our decisions have consequences. It empowers us to make deliberate choices and act in harmony with our core values and goals.

Let's meet someone named Maya. She's always had a dream of becoming a writer. One day, she decided to take a writing class. That one choice sets off a chain of events: she meets fellow aspiring writers, finds a mentor, and eventually publishes her own book. The cause (joining the writing class) leads to the effect (publishing a book), shaping the course of her life.

Crafting Our Reality:

Imagine you're a builder, creating the structure of your life one brick at a time. Every choice, thought and intention you have is like a brick that shapes the grand design of your existence. You're at the centre of this cause-and-effect symphony, constructing the building towards your chosen design.

The Power of Energy and Vibration:

Indeed, everything in our world is comprised of energy and vibrations. At the smallest level, we find atoms, and even they are not still; they're in constant motion. This perpetual movement characterizes them as forms of energy vibrating at various frequencies. This fundamental concept, rooted in the field of quantum mechanics, highlights the dynamic nature of our universe and lays the foundation for understanding how energy and vibrations influence the reality we perceive.

Consider how your energy and vibes affect your experiences. Just like musical instruments create different notes based on their vibrations, your thoughts and actions send out vibrations that shape your reality. Your energy becomes the fertile soil where circumstances take root.

Embracing the Power of Choice:

There's a significant shift that happens when you embrace responsibility for your life. By understanding that you are both the cause and effect of your reality, you regain control of your destiny. Each thought, intention, and action becomes a brushstroke on the canvas of your life. Each choice you make can have a profound impact on your life. Often better results are as simple as making better choices. Making the right choices means that you will live a life of choice and not chance. You have the ability to choose, choose to win.

Moulding Reality through Vibration:

Imagine how adjusting your personal vibration can change the canvas of your existence. When you elevate your energy and alter your vibration, the threads of your reality adjust to match this new resonance. You become the conductor, harmonizing the orchestra of cause and effect. Nothing works from a low energy, everything works better from a high energy.

Imagine energy as the fuel that powers your endeavours in life. It's like the electricity that lights up a room. When your energy is low, it's as if you're trying to illuminate a vast space with a dim, flickering light bulb. Your efforts become sluggish, and tasks seem more daunting.

However, when you operate from a high-energy state, it's akin to having a floodlight that can illuminate the entire area brilliantly. Everything you do is infused with vigour, clarity, and effectiveness.

Low Energy: You wake up feeling tired and uninspired. Your thoughts are clouded with negativity, and you lack enthusiasm for the day ahead. As you approach your work, you find it difficult to concentrate, and tasks seem to drag on forever. You make mistakes and miss deadlines, and overall, the quality of your work is subpar. In conversations, you lack charisma and struggle to connect with others.

High Energy: Contrast this with a day when you wake up feeling energized, focused, and motivated. Your thoughts are positive, and you're excited about your goals. As you tackle your tasks, you're in a state of flow. Your productivity soars and you effortlessly complete your work to a high standard. In conversations, you radiate charisma and connect deeply with others.

The key takeaway is that your energy state can profoundly impact your effectiveness in various aspects of life. When your energy is high, you're more creative, efficient, and capable of overcoming challenges. It's not just about physical energy; it also encompasses your mental and emotional states.

Therefore, nurturing and maintaining high energy levels through practices like regular exercise, meditation, positive thinking, and a healthy lifestyle can significantly enhance your performance and overall quality of life.

The Symphony of Self-Creation:

Envision the universe as a grand symphony, with you as the conductor. As you change and fine-tune your personal vibration, the instruments of reality respond, creating a symphony of events that resonate with your desires. You become the nexus of cause and effect, shaping the very composition of your life.

Unleashing Infinite Possibilities:

Within this understanding lies the limitless potential that emerges when you grasp the profound interplay of cause and effect. By embracing your role as both the architect and sculptor of your reality, you open the door to a world of boundless opportunities.

Harmonizing with the Universal Symphony:

Imagine living in harmony with the grand dance of cause and

effect in the universe. By weaving your intentions and actions into this eternal tapestry, you align yourself with the universal currents, co-creating a reality that echoes your highest aspirations.

As we journeed through Chapter 6, we explored the rich tapestry of universal laws surrounding us, recognizing our role as both recipients and agents of cause and effect. By understanding that our thoughts, actions, and intentions are the threads that weave the fabric of our existence, we step into the powerful realm of conscious creation and transformation.

Chapter 7: The Six Laws of the Mind

Your subconscious mind is like fertile soil which accepts any seed you plant within it. Your habitual thoughts and beliefs are the seeds which are being constantly sown within, and they produce in your life what is planted just as surely as corn kernels produce corn. You will reap what you sow.

This is a law.

- John Kehoe

In the realm of personal development and self-mastery, there exists a profound understanding of the intricacies that govern our mental landscape. These are the Six Laws of the Mind, each a cornerstone of our inner world and a compass guiding us on our journey of transformation. As we embark on this exploration, we open the doors to harnessing the full potential of our thoughts and emotions, ultimately shaping the reality we desire.

The First Law: Thoughts Are Real Forces

One of the foundational principles that govern our mental realm is the First Law of the Mind: Thoughts are real forces that set a cause in motion. This law draws parallels to scientific concepts, such as Einstein's theory of relativity ($E=MC^2$), highlighting that thoughts are energy and vibrations with the potential to shape our reality.

With this principle in mind, you embark on a journey to understand that you are the culmination of your thoughts and beliefs. The power to transform your life resides within your ability to direct your thoughts purposefully and intentionally, thereby influencing your energy and vibrations. Every thought is an energy and a vibration.

In our mental world, something remarkable is at play: thoughts are not just passing ideas, they are like powerful tools. These thoughts hold a unique strength that can genuinely change the course of our lives. Imagine them as seeds you plant; they grow into the reality you experience.

How It Works in Daily Life:

Consider this in your everyday life. When you think positively, like "I can do it," or "I'll have a good day," it often leads to positive outcomes. You feel more confident, and others respond positively to you. It's like a ripple effect of good things.

On the flip side, if you're constantly thinking negatively, like "I'll never succeed," or "Everything is going wrong," it can become a self-fulfilling prophecy. You might lack motivation, and others may perceive you as negative, which can create a cycle of negativity.

So, this law reminds us to be mindful of our thoughts because they have real power. Like a sculptor with clay, we mould our lives with our thoughts. By choosing positive ones, we shape a brighter future.

The Second Law: The Mind as a Sending and Receiving Station of Thought

Now, picture your mind as a powerful transmitter, like a two-way radio. It doesn't just generate thoughts; it sends and receives them too. This law highlights that our minds are all connected in a vast web of consciousness. The thoughts we send out don't just vanish; they become part of a larger pattern that influences not only our individual lives but also the collective human experience.

How It Works in Daily Life:

Think about it this way. When you're feeling happy and optimistic, those emotions aren't just confined to your own little bubble. They radiate outward and can affect people around you. Have you ever noticed how being around a positive person can brighten your day?

Conversely, when you're around someone who's angry or upset, you might start feeling tense or agitated too. It's like you're picking up on their emotional "transmission."

So, this law reminds us that our thoughts and emotions don't just stay inside our heads. They're like radio signals, influencing not only our own experiences but also the wider world. Being aware of this interconnectedness can help us contribute positively to the collective consciousness.

Breaking Free from the Chains of External Validation

In the realm of self-development, a powerful adversary often emerges with the incessant need for external validation. Let's peel back the layers of this formidable challenge, delving into the Second Law of the Mind and offering insights to liberate your thoughts and actions from the grip of seeking approval from others.

Understanding the Second Law of the Mind: The Radiating Influence of Thought:

The Second Law of the Mind states that the mind is both a sending and receiving station of thought. It underscores the notion that our thoughts and focus can attract corresponding energies and outcomes. This law reveals the profound connection between our mental states and the reality we create.

The Struggle of Seeking External Validation: The Fear Within:

The primal emotion of fear often cloaks itself in disguises, none more deceptive than the fear of judgment and the quest for external approval.

This fear arises from the false belief that others' opinions hold more weight than our own desires and convictions. It's a fear rooted in False Evidence Appearing Real (FEAR).

The Irony of Caring Too Much: A Self-Fulfilling Prophecy:

Ironically, the very act of caring excessively about others' opinions can lead to diminished self-respect and the erosion of the traits we seek to protect. This self-defeating cycle restricts our actions, stifles our authenticity, and constrains our personal growth.

The Paralysis of People-Pleasing: A Limiting Existence:

The relentless pursuit of pleasing others often blinds us to our true aspirations. We say yes to engagements and commitments that align with the expectations of others, leaving little room for pursuing endeavours that resonate with our passions and values. This stifling cycle ultimately impedes our personal evolution and life's fulfilment.

Breaking free from the clutches of external validation entails cultivating a heroic mindset. This mindset strikes the balance between compassion and personal authenticity. It involves prioritizing others' happiness while detaching from the need for their approval. By adopting this perspective, we can engage in selfless actions and embrace our true selves simultaneously.

The key to unshackling ourselves from the allure of external validation lies in nurturing a sense of inner validation. The path involves setting personal standards and adhering to a self-constructed code of conduct. By striving to be the best version of ourselves each day, we shift our focus from comparing ourselves to others to honouring our unique journey.

Cultivating an Authentic Existence: Your Race, Your Rules:

Life's race is not a competition with others; it's a journey of self-discovery and personal growth. The pursuit of external validation can shackle our potential, while a commitment to internal validation paves the way for an authentic, fulfilling life. By shedding the chains of caring too much about what others think, we liberate ourselves to become the architects of our own reality—one that is defined by authenticity, courage, and personal mastery.

The Third Law: The Law of Attraction

Thoughts that are emotionalised become magnetised and attract similar and like thoughts. Where focus goes energy flows. We get what we focus on.

By understanding this law, we gain insight into the profound connection between our emotional responses and the outcomes they attract.

How It Works in Daily Life:

Think about your thoughts and emotions as magnets. When you think about something and add strong emotions to it, it's like supercharging that thought. It becomes a powerful magnet, attracting more thoughts and situations that are alike.

For example, if you often think about success and truly believe in it, you'll attract conditions and circumstances that align with your thoughts. You might notice opportunities that you didn't see before, and things seem to work out in your favour. That's because your predominant thought patterns are shaping your reality.

Conversely, if you dwell on negative thoughts and let fear or doubt dominate your thinking, those thoughts become magnets for more negativity. You might find yourself stuck in a cycle of challenges and setbacks because your predominant thoughts are attracting such circumstances.

So, the Law of Attraction is a reminder that every thought, especially when it's filled with emotion, has the power to become a magnet, drawing in similar thoughts and shaping your reality accordingly. By consciously choosing positive thoughts and beliefs, you can create a reality that aligns with your desires and aspirations. It's like being the architect of your own life.

The Fourth Law: The Law of Control

Now, let's explore the fourth law, which is all about control, but not in the way you might think.

How It Works in Daily Life:

Imagine you have a superpower, the power of control, not over the external world, but over your own thoughts and emotions. This is what the Law of Control is all about.

In life, many things are beyond our control. We can't control the weather, other people's actions, or unexpected events. But here's the game-changer: we can control how we react to all these things. It's like having a superpower.

Think of it as a ship sailing through a storm. You can't control the storm itself, but you can control how you steer your ship. In the same way, you can choose how you respond to life's challenges. This is where your power lies.

By mastering this law, you become the captain of your own emotional ship. You can navigate through life's ups and downs with grace and poise. You can shape your emotional landscape to match your intentions. When challenges arise, you don't react impulsively; instead, you respond thoughtfully.

For example, if you face a difficult situation, like a disagreement with a colleague at work, you have a choice. You can react with anger and frustration, which might escalate the situation. Or, you can choose to respond with calm and empathy, finding a solution together. Your ability to control your reactions can turn a potential conflict into a positive outcome.

So, the Law of Control empowers you to be the master of your own emotional world. It's like having a remote control for your reactions, and by using it wisely, you can shape your life according to your intentions.

The Fifth Law: The Law of Insertion

The fifth law is all about inserting positivity into your mind. It's like planting seeds of success and growth. We have the power to insert any thought of any type into our minds. Your real wealth and security lies in the ability to think whatever you choose. You must however train your mind to think in new ways.

How It Works in Daily Life:

Think of your mind as a garden. In this garden, you have both flowers (positive thoughts) and weeds (negative thoughts). The Law of Insertion is like planting more flowers and pulling out the weeds.

Imagine you have a belief that says, "I'm not good at public speaking." This belief is like a weed in your mental garden. It limits you and holds you back.

Now, here's where the Law of Insertion comes in. You consciously decide to plant a new thought, like, "I am becoming a confident speaker." This new thought is like planting a beautiful flower.

Every time you repeat this positive thought, it's as if you're watering and nurturing that flower. With time and repetition, it grows stronger and begins to crowd out the weeds.

This law acknowledges that you have the power to change your beliefs by deliberately introducing positive thoughts. By doing this, you're reprogramming your mental canvas. You're nurturing the seeds of possibility and growth.

For instance, if you want to start a new business but have doubts, you can insert positive thoughts like, "I have the skills and determination to succeed," or "Every challenge is an opportunity for growth." As you water these thoughts daily through repetition, they take root and become your new beliefs.

So, the Law of Insertion is like being a gardener of your own mind. You can choose to cultivate positivity, and over time, it will blossom and transform your beliefs, ultimately shaping your reality.

Law 6: The Law of Connection: Harmonizing Your Inner and Outer Worlds

In the intricate fabric of life, your inner world, filled with thoughts and feelings, is tightly woven with the outer world, where your experiences unfold. The inner world creates the outer world once you stop reacting to the outer world and start creating in the inner world.

How It Works in Daily Life:

Have you ever noticed that when you're in a good mood, good things seem to happen more often? Or when you're feeling down, it's like a cloud follows you? This is the Law of Connection at play.

Picture this: your inner thoughts and emotions are like a loom, and the threads you weave with them shape your life's fabric. If you weave threads of positivity, gratitude, and abundance, your life's tapestry becomes beautiful.

Now, here's the magic: the Law of Connection works both ways. Just as your inner world influences your outer world, the outer world can affect your inner state. For example, a walk in a serene park can make you feel peaceful, or a kind word from a stranger can brighten your day. It's like your outer world becomes a canvas where your inner experiences are painted.

But here's where it gets interesting. You have control over this exchange. By filling your inner world with positivity, you create a filter. This filter makes you notice the beauty and opportunities in the outer world. It's like wearing glasses that highlight the good stuff.

So, the Law of Connection turns you into an alchemist of your reality. Your thoughts become experiences, your emotions shape your encounters, and your intentions mould your outcomes. As you flow between your inner and outer worlds, you realize that you have the power to create a beautiful tapestry of life.

In simpler terms, think of your thoughts and emotions as tools. If you use positive tools, you create a more positive life. And by focusing on the good things around you, you make your life even better. This law reminds us that our inner and outer worlds are connected, and we can make that connection work in our favour.

Chapter 8: The Busy Conscious Mind: Taming the Thought Jungle

It is only through your conscious mind that you can reach the subconscious. Your conscious mind is the porter at the door, the watchman at the gate. It is to the conscious mind that the subconscious looks for all its impressions.

- Robert Collier

Imagine your conscious mind as a bustling marketplace. In this marketplace, thoughts are like people passing by. Some of these thoughts are like helpful friends offering valuable advice, while others are like noisy street vendors trying to sell you things you don't need. Your daily experiences, concerns, and even worries are like the activity in this busy marketplace.

Observing Your Mental Street

Throughout the day, it's essential to pause and observe this mental street. You can do this several times a day. Imagine stepping back and watching your thoughts as if you're watching people in a bustling market square. Be curious, be detached, as if you're observing someone else's thoughts and not your own.

Validating Your Thoughts

As you observe, validate your thoughts. Are they true? Are they false? Or are you unsure? Just like you'd evaluate the quality of items in a market, evaluate the quality of your thoughts. Some thoughts might be useful, like a fresh fruit stand with ripe ideas, while others might be rotten, like spoiled food you should avoid.

Weeding the Negative Thoughts

Negative thoughts are like weeds in your mental garden. Daily, you can practice getting rid of them. Here are a few techniques:

Cut It Off: When you catch a negative thought, cut it off immediately. Replace it with a different, better thought. It's like pulling out a weed and planting a beautiful flower in its place. For example, if you think, "I'll never be good at this," replace it with, "I can learn and improve."

Label It: Call it what it is—a negative thought. Naming it takes away some of its power. Imagine putting a sign on a noisy vendor that says "Noisemaker." By recognizing it as negative, you gain control over it.

Exaggerate It: Sometimes, negative thoughts are irrational. Exaggerate them to the point of absurdity. If your mind says, "I'll mess up everything," picture yourself creating a comically exaggerated disaster. This helps you realize the thought's irrationality.

Counteract It: Replace the negative thought with the exact opposite. Your mind can only focus on one thought at a time. If your thought is, "I'm a failure," shift it to, "I am capable and can succeed."

The Power of Concentration

Concentration is like training your inner mental muscles. It's about focusing on one thought or concept to the exclusion of others. Just like in a crowded marketplace, you can choose to focus on a single item. Concentration exercises your mind's ability to direct its attention intentionally.

Example:

Imagine you're about to give a presentation, and a negative thought pops up: "I'm going to mess up, and everyone will laugh at me." Here's how you can apply these techniques:

Cut It Off: Stop that thought in its tracks. Replace it with a positive affirmation: "I've prepared well, and I'll do my best."

Label It: Say to yourself, "Ah, there's that negative thought again, trying to make me anxious." By recognizing it, you regain control.

Exaggerate It: Take that negative thought and make it ridiculous. Imagine yourself doing a wild and hilarious dance on stage while everyone applauds. This helps you see the thought's irrationality.

Counteract It: Replace the negative thought with the opposite:

"I'm confident, and my presentation will be a success." Visualize a positive outcome.

Remember, negative thoughts only have power over you if you entertain them. By observing, validating, and weeding out the negativity, you exercise your mental muscles. Over time, your mind naturally becomes less negative because you're focusing on what truly matters. Like tending to a garden, with patience and practice, your mental street becomes a more pleasant place to stroll.

Chapter 9: The Farmer's Wisdom: Embracing the Perspective of "Good, Bad, Who Really Knows?"

Train your mind to see the good in everything. Positivity is a choice. The happiness of your life depends on the quality of your thoughts.

- Marc & Angel Chernoff

In a world where events and circumstances often defy easy categorization as "good" or "bad," the story of the farmer and his horse serves as a profound reminder of the power of perspective. This tale, rooted in ancient wisdom, invites us to explore the nuanced and ever-changing nature of life's experiences, challenging us to reevaluate our habitual judgments and interpretations.

The Horse's Disappearance: The Unforeseen Shifts of Life:

Amid the tranquillity of a faraway village, the farmer awakens one fateful day to discover that his cherished horse has vanished without a trace. An unexpected loss that could evoke sorrow and despair prompts the farmer to utter a seemingly simple yet profound phrase: "good, bad, who knows?" In this moment, he demonstrates a remarkable capacity to transcend immediate emotional reactions and remain open to the unfolding of events.

The Arrival of the Brumbies: The Complexity of Fortune:

Weeks later, an astonishing turn of events occurs—the farmer's horse returns, accompanied by eleven wild brumbies. The addition of these new horses could be perceived as a boon, yet the farmer's response remains unaltered: "good, bad, who knows?" Here, the farmer illustrates the value of withholding judgment and embracing the multifaceted nature of circumstances. By refraining from hasty categorization, he avoids falling into the trap of viewing events in black-and-white terms.

The Tragedy and the War: Finding Wisdom in Adversity:

In a stark twist of fate, the farmer's son meets an unfortunate accident while taming one of the brumbies, resulting in paralysis. In the eyes of the community, this is a heartbreaking tragedy, yet the farmer responds with his characteristic refrain: "good, bad, who knows?" This poignant example illustrates the farmer's resilience in the face of adversity and his recognition that the ultimate implications of any event are far-reaching and intricate.

The Unforeseen Blessings: Beyond the Veil of Judgment:

As war engulfs the nation and the spectre of conscription looms, the farmer's son is spared due to his paralysis. A conventional viewpoint might label this as a fortunate turn of events, but the farmer's unwavering response remains unchanged: "good, bad, who really knows?" His perspective exemplifies the ability to perceive silver linings even amidst circumstances that may initially appear unfavourable.

The Power of Perspective: A Profound Lesson:

At the heart of this timeless story lies the essential truth that events themselves lack inherent value judgments; rather, our interpretations mould them into experiences of good or bad. The farmer's sagacious repetition of "good, bad, who knows" serves as a touchstone for cultivating an open-minded and non-reactive approach to life's ever-evolving tapestry.

Tom Ziglar's Insight: Shaping Our Reality:

The resonance between the farmer's wisdom and Tom Ziglar's assertion that the state of business is determined "between your ears" underscores the profound influence of our perspective on shaping our reality. Just as the farmer transcends the immediate and labels events with broader strokes, so too can we shape our lives by adopting perspectives that align with our inner truths.

The Wisdom of Equanimity:

I want to encourage you to embrace the wisdom of the farmer's philosophy—of embracing life's fluidity with equanimity. By relinquishing the urge to impose rigid labels on events, we liberate ourselves from the shackles of judgment. We become free to experience the vast spectrum of human experiences without being confined by preconceived notions. As we navigate the intricate dance of existence, we are invited to embody the timeless refrain: "good, bad, who really knows?"

Chapter 10: The Power of the Spoken Word

Words, like seeds, find fertile ground in our hearts, not on the barren earth. Plant them wisely, for one day you may dine upon the harvest of your speech.

- Steyn Rossouw

In our exploration of the incredible potential of the mind, we've delved into the realms of thought, emotion, and visualization. Now, we venture into the tangible world of words, the bridge between the ethereal and the material. This chapter reveals the profound impact of the spoken word on your mind's power and your ability to shape your reality. When your thoughts, actions, and words are in alignment, you unlock a potent force often referred to as "the magic of alignment." Here's a closer look at why this alignment is so powerful:

The Magic of Alignment and The Spoken Word

In the grand symphony of life, there exists a powerful harmony between your thoughts, actions, and the words you speak. This chapter explores the profound connection between aligning these three elements, often referred to as "the magic of alignment," and harnessing the spoken word as a manifestation tool.

When your thoughts, actions, and words are in harmony, a potent force is awakened within you, "the magic of alignment". This chapter will look deeper into how you can use this manifestation tool.

Let's delve into why this alignment is so potent:

Alignment brings clarity. Your thoughts, in sync with your desires, guide your actions, ensuring purposeful progress towards your goals.

Aligned actions reveal your commitment to your objectives. They shield you from distractions, keeping your gaze fixed firmly on your targets.

Aligned words and actions emit a consistent, positive energy. This energy attracts similar vibrations from the universe, aligning external circumstances with your inner intentions.

Alignment encourages authenticity. You express your true self, forging authentic connections with others.

Alignment makes you magnetic. Belief in your goals, positive words, and actions in line with them turn you into a magnet for opportunities and resources.

Aligning thoughts, words, and actions empowers you. It reinforces belief in your abilities, boosting confidence and self-esteem.

Practical Steps for Alignment:

Mindfulness: Cultivate self-awareness to ensure your thoughts and feelings align with your goals.

Positive Affirmations: Use affirmations to align thoughts and words with your desires.

Visualization: Combine words and mental imagery to sharpen focus on your desired outcomes.

Consistent Action: Take daily actions, regardless of size, that align with your goals.

Positive Self-Talk: Replace self-doubt with self-compassion through spoken affirmations.

Integrity: Align actions with your values and principles.

Remember, achieving alignment is an ongoing process. Routinely assess your thoughts, words, and actions to maintain congruence with your aspirations. When you master alignment, you unleash a transformative force that propels you towards your dreams, creating a life brimming with purpose and fulfilment.

The Spoken Word as a Manifestation Tool:

Every word you speak has the power to shape your reality. Uttering thoughts aloud transforms them into tangible expressions, marking a vital step in the manifestation process.

1. Clarity and Focus:

Speaking your intentions clarifies your desires, sharpening your focus and commitment to achieving them.

2. Affirmations:

Words, spoken with conviction, are potent transformation tools. Affirmations reinforce desired beliefs and outcomes.

3. Self-Talk:

Monitor self-talk—the internal dialogue. Transform it into a positive, encouraging force, nurturing self-compassion and self-worth.

Daily Self-Talk Exercise

Inspiration for this Self Talk Exercise was derived from the wisdom and teaching of Zig Ziglar, whose insights continue to empower and uplift countless individuals.

I, _____, am honest, intelligent and organized.

I am a responsible, committed and teachable person who is sober and loyal.

I clearly understand that regardless of who signs my pay cheque I am self-employed.

I am an optimistic, punctual, enthusiastic, goal-setting, smart working self-starter.

I am disciplined, focused and dependable.

I am a persistent positive thinker with great self-control.

I am an energetic and diligent team player and hard worker who appreciates the opportunity my company and the free enterprise system offer me.

I am thrifty with my resources and apply common sense to my daily tasks. I take honest pride in my competence, appearance and manners.

I am motivated to be and do my best so that my healthy self-image will remain on solid ground.

These are the qualities which enable me to manage myself and help give me employment security in a no-job-security world.

I, _____, am a compassionate, respectful encourager who is considerate.

I am generous and gentle. I am a patient, caring, sensitive, attentive, fun-loving person.

I am a supportive, giving forgiving, kind, unselfish and affectionate human being.

I am a sincere and open-minded good listener and a good-finder who is trustworthy.

These are the qualities which enable me to build good relationships with my associates, neighbours, friends and family.

I, _____, am a person of integrity, with the faith and wisdom to know what I should do and the courage and convictions to follow through.

I have the vision to manage myself and to lead others. I am authoritative, confident, and humbly grateful for the opportunity life offers me.

I am fair, flexible, resourceful and creative. I am knowledgeable, decisive and an extra-miler with a servant's attitude who communicates well with others.

I am a consistent, pragmatic teacher with character and a finely-tuned sense of humour.

I am an honourable person and am balanced in my personal, family and business life. I have a passion for being, doing and learning more today so I can be, do and have more tomorrow.

These are the qualities of the winner I was born to be, and I am fully committed to developing these marvellous qualities with which I have been entrusted. Tonight, I'm going to sleep wonderfully well. I will dream powerful, positive dreams. I always remember my dreams. I will awaken energized and refreshed. Tomorrow's going to be magnificent and my future is unlimited. Recognizing, claiming and developing these qualities which I already have, gives me a legitimate chance to be happier, healthier, more prosperous, more secure, have more friends, greater peace of mind, better family relationships and legitimate hope that the future will be even better."

Repeat the process the next morning and close by saying, "These are the qualities of the winner I was born to be, and I will develop and use these qualities to achieve my worthy objectives. Today is a brand new day and it's mine to use in a marvellously productive way."

After 30 days, add the next step:

Choose your strongest quality and the one you feel needs the most work.

Example: Strongest—honest.
            Needs most work—organized.

On a separate 3x5 card, print "I, _____, am a completely honest person and every day I am getting better and better organized."

Keep this 3x5 card handy and read it out loud at every

opportunity for one week. Repeat this process with the second strongest quality and the second one which needs the most work. Do this until you've completed the entire list. Use this self-talk procedure as long as you want to get more of the things money will buy and all of the things money won't buy.

Note: Because of some painful experiences in the past (betrayal, abuse, etc.), there might be a word or two that brings back unpleasant memories (for example: discipline). Eliminate the word or substitute another word.

4. Declarations:

Boldly declare your intentions, announcing them to the universe. This self-assertion ignites the energy required for manifestation.

5. Visualization Enhancement:

Combine spoken words with visualization, describing goals vividly as you visualize them. This multi-sensory approach intensifies mental imagery's power.

The Vibrational Nature of Words:

Words are not just carriers of ideas; they're vibrations with unique energy signatures. Positive words resonate with high frequencies, attracting positivity. Choose words wisely, for they reflect their meanings' energies.

Practical Exercises for Harnessing the Spoken Word:

Daily Affirmations: Create a list of affirmations reflecting your goals and recite them each morning for a positive start.

Declaration Ritual: Dedicate a specific time daily to declare intentions confidently and with conviction.

Gratitude Journal: Maintain a journal where you express gratitude, amplifying appreciation for life's positives.

Positive Self-Talk: Replace self-criticism with self-empower-ment, speaking to yourself as you would to a cherished friend.

Conclusion:

The spoken word is a dynamic tool for manifesting desires and nurturing a positive mindset. Harness its power using affirmations, declarations, and positive self-talk. As you speak with clarity and conviction, you amplify the vibrational energy of your intentions, aligning reality with your desires. Your words are not just expressions; they are the incantations that shape your world. Embrace this magic of alignment and watch as your dreams take form in the tapestry of your life.

Chapter 11: Mastering Your Mind: Daily Rituals for Harnessing Thought Power

You'll never change your life until you change something you do daily. The secret of your success is found in your daily routine."

\- John C. Maxwell

In this chapter, we will delve deep into creating a daily routine that harnesses the incredible power of your thoughts. This routine isn't just about understanding the concepts; it's about implementing them consistently to create lasting change. By embracing these daily practices, you will develop the habit of thought mastery, unlocking your true potential.

1. Consciously Begin Your Day:

Imagine awakening each morning with the awareness that your first thought sets the tone for your entire day. This is the moment when you consciously choose the direction of your thoughts. Instead of letting random and often negative thoughts dictate your mood, you take control.

As you wake, before even getting out of bed, take a few moments to reflect on something positive in your life. It could be the warmth of your blanket, the prospect of a new day, or the love of your family. By consistently doing this, you're training your mind to start the day with positivity. I love to control my first thought of the day as I become aware that I am awake I tell myself that I am truly thankful for the love, joy and abundance that surround me every day. I believe this sets the tone for the day and that the attitude of gratitude is the most powerful of all human emotions.

2. Embrace Gratitude:

Gratitude is a transformative practice that shifts your focus from what's lacking in your life to the abundance that surrounds you.

Things you can do to practice gratitude daily include:

Gratitude Journal: Dedicate a few minutes each morning to jot down three things you're grateful for. They can range from the simple pleasures of life to the profound connections you cherish.

Express Appreciation: Don't just feel gratitude; express it. Tell someone important to you why you appreciate them. This act of acknowledgement not only brightens their day but also deepens their own sense of gratitude.

Connect with Nature: Spend a few minutes outdoors, absorbing the beauty of the natural world. Whether it's the colours of the sunrise, the rustling leaves, or the songs of the birds, nature offers a profound source of gratitude.

3. Set Daily Intentions:

The power of intention lies in its ability to direct your focus and energy. Where focus goes energy flows. When you begin your day with clear intentions, you establish a roadmap for your thoughts and actions. The magic lies in getting our thoughts, words and actions into alignment.

Before diving into your daily tasks, take a moment to ask yourself, "What do I want to achieve today? What actions can I take to move closer to my goals?" This practice ensures that your thoughts and efforts are purposeful and aligned with your aspirations.

4. Contemplation: A Deep Dive into Thought:

Contemplation involves self-reflection and gaining deeper insights into your inner world.

Contemplation is like taking a deep dive into the ocean of your thoughts. It's a mental exercise that serves two significant purposes: it strengthens your mind and enhances your understanding of the subject you're contemplating.

Developing Mental Fitness:

Think of your mind as a muscle. Just as you lift weights to strengthen your body, you contemplate to enhance your mental fitness. Contemplation requires focus, patience, and concentration, which are like the workouts for your brain. The more you practice, the more your mental muscles grow.

Gaining Profound Insight:

Contemplation isn't just about exercising your mind; it's also a journey toward deeper understanding. When you contemplate a concept or idea, you're like a detective examining every nook and cranny. You dissect it, consider its implications, and explore it from all angles. This process leads to profound insights and a greater grasp of the subject.

Contemplation Exercise Example:

Let's say you want to contemplate the concept of time. Here's a step-by-step exercise:

Choose Your Focus: Start by selecting the idea or concept you want to contemplate. In this case, it's time.

Dive In Deep: Immerse yourself in the concept. Ponder what time means to you and society as a whole. Think about how it influences your daily life and the world around you.

Stay Committed: Sometimes, your mind might resist and say, "This is boring." Ignore that voice and stay with the concept. Continue to explore it, even if it seems repetitive.

Ask Questions: Challenge yourself by asking questions about time. What are its different dimensions? How does it affect your past, present, and future? How do various cultures perceive time?

Repetition is Key: Finally, repeat the process. Go over your contemplation again and again, like revisiting a favourite book. With each repetition, you'll uncover new layers of understanding.

In the end, contemplation is like a mental gym where you work out your mind, making it stronger and more flexible. It's also a treasure hunt for knowledge, where you dig deep to uncover hidden gems of insight. So, whether you're contemplating time, a philosophical concept or any other idea, remember that the journey of contemplation is as rewarding as the destination.

Dedicate a few minutes daily to contemplate your life's direction. Reflect on your core values, identify your strengths, and acknowledge areas for personal growth. This introspection enhances self-awareness, a cornerstone of thought mastery.

Daily Seeding: Planting the Seeds of Your Desires

Seeding is like planting the seeds of your desires in the fertile soil of your mind. It's a powerful technique where you focus your thoughts intensely on a specific idea, holding it in your mind to the exclusion of all others. The key to seeding is to convince your inner world that you already possess what you desire, and it's a practice that involves both imagination and emotion.

Claiming Possession:

Imagine you have a garden, and you're planting seeds for beautiful flowers. In seeding, the thought you hold is that you already have the things you desire. It's like claiming ownership in the inner world. You don't just think about it; you become it.

Feeling the Reality:

To start, ask yourself, "What would it feel like to have what I want?" Use your imagination to paint a vivid mental picture. Imagine you already have that dream job, that loving relationship, or that sense of inner peace.

Vibrating with Emotion:

Now, it's time to dive deeper. Feel it through your entire body. Close your eyes, relax, and soak in the feeling. If it's a sense of achievement, let that emotion wash over you. If it's love, embrace the warmth and joy it brings. The key is to vibrate with the feeling as if it's real because, in your inner world, it is.

Making it Real:

Claim it now, not in the distant future. Seeding is about making your desires a present reality in your mind. When you engage with this practice regularly, you align your thoughts and emotions with your aspirations.

For example, if your desire is financial abundance, imagine the freedom, security, and excitement it brings. Feel the weight of money in your hand, the joy of giving, and the ease of financial decisions. These sensations aren't just in your mind; they're in your whole being.

Remember, daily seeding is a way to cultivate a mindset of abundance, success, and fulfilment. The more you practice, the more your inner world aligns with your desires. It's like tending to a garden: with patience, consistency, and belief, you'll see the seeds of your desires bloom into reality. So, claim what you want now, and let it grow within you.

Visualization: Painting Your Desired Reality and the Power of Vision Boards

Visualization is like having a mental movie screen where you can project your dreams and aspirations. It's a powerful tool for shaping your thoughts, enhancing belief in your abilities, and strengthening your commitment to your goals. One way to supercharge your visualization practice is by creating a vision board.

Creating Mental Images:

Start by closing your eyes and picturing the desired outcome. Whether it's acing that big presentation, finding your dream home, or achieving inner peace, see it clearly in your mind's eye. Visualize the details—what you see, hear, and feel in this moment of success.

Embracing Emotions:

But it's not just about images; it's about feelings. Imagine the sense of accomplishment, the joy, and the pride that comes with reaching your goal. Feel these emotions as if they are happening right now. This emotional connection is key to making your visualization powerful.

Boosting Belief:

Visualization is like a confidence booster. As you repeatedly visualize your success, your mind begins to accept it as a reality. Doubts and insecurities gradually fade away, replaced by a deep belief in your capabilities.

Enhancing Commitment:

Moreover, visualization reinforces your commitment to your goals. It's like a mental rehearsal for success. When you see yourself accomplishing your desires repeatedly, it becomes a part of your inner world. This, in turn, drives you to take real-world actions that bring you closer to your goals.

Vision Boards: Turning Dreams Into Reality

Now, let's introduce the concept of vision boards. A vision board is a physical representation of your goals and desires. It's a collage of images, words, and symbols that visually depict what you want to achieve. Here's why they work:

1. Visual Reinforcement: Vision boards keep your goals in plain sight. When you see your aspirations every day, it reminds you of what you're working towards. It's like having a visual cue that constantly reinforces your commitment.

2. Clarity: Creating a vision board forces you to clarify your goals. You need to choose images and words that represent your desires clearly. This process helps you define what you truly want.

3. Focus: Your vision board acts as a focal point for your daily visualization. It's a tangible representation of your dreams that you can easily access. When you look at it, you immediately dive into your visualization practice.

How to Create a Vision Board:

Gather Materials: Collect magazines, newspapers, images, and any other materials that resonate with your goals.

Define Your Goals: Before you start, be clear about your objectives. What do you want to achieve? What areas of your life do you want to improve?

Select Images and Words. Go through your materials and choose images and words that represent your goals. They should evoke strong positive emotions.

Create Your Board: Get a large poster board or corkboard. Arrange and glue your chosen images and words onto the board in a way that's visually appealing to you.

Place Your Board: Put your vision board in a location where you'll see it every day, like your bedroom or workspace.

Regularly Visualize: Spend time each day in front of your vision board, visualizing the success and happiness associated with your goals.

By combining visualization with a vision board, you're not only creating mental images of your desires, but you're also giving them a physical presence in your life. It's a dynamic approach to manifesting your dreams, reinforcing your commitment, and turning your aspirations into reality.

Daily Affirmations: Nurturing the Positive Within You

Affirmations are like gentle whispers of encouragement to your subconscious mind. They are positive statements that reinforce your beliefs, boost your self-esteem, and help you stay aligned with your goals. By repeating affirmations daily, you can harness the power of your thoughts to shape your reality. Here are some personal mastery daily affirmations that can inspire and uplift you:

Gratitude: "I am deeply thankful for the abundance, the joy, and the love that surrounds me every day."

Empowerment: "I am the architect of my life; I build its foundation and choose its contents."

Energy and Joy: "Today, I am brimming with energy and overflowing with joy."

Health and Well-being: "My body is healthy; my mind is brilliant; my soul is tranquil."

Positivity: "I am superior to negative thoughts and low actions."

Talents and Creativity: "I have been given endless talents which I am utilizing every day."

Compassion and Love: "A river of compassion washes away my anger and replaces it with love."

Guidance and Protection: "I am guided, directed, and protected."

Marriage and Relationships: "(If you're married) My marriage is becoming stronger, deeper, and more stable every day in every way."

Success: "I possess the qualities needed to be extremely successful."

Business: "(For business owners) My business is growing, expanding, and thriving."

Creativity: "Creative energy surges through me and leads me to new and brilliant ideas."

Happiness: "Happiness is a choice. I base my happiness on my own accomplishments and the blessings I've been given."

Overcoming Challenges: "My ability to conquer my challenges is limitless; my potential to succeed is infinite."

Positive Thoughts: "My thoughts are filled with positivity, and my life is plentiful with prosperity."

Positive Change: "Today, I abandon my old habits and take up new, more positive ones."

Admiration: "Many people look up to me and recognize my worth; I am admired."

Family and Friends: "I am blessed with an incredible family and wonderful friends."

Self-Worth: "I acknowledge my own self-worth; my confidence is soaring."

Self-Improvement: "Every day in every way I am getting better and better."

Inner Strength: "I am a powerhouse; I am indestructible."

Visualizing Success: "My future is an ideal projection of what I envision now."

Manifestation: "My efforts are being supported by the universe; my dreams manifest into reality before my eyes."

Radiance: "I radiate beauty, charm, and grace."

Health: "Every day in every way I am getting healthier and healthier."

Strength: "I wake up today with strength in my heart and clarity in my mind."

Freedom from Fear: "My fears of tomorrow are simply melting away."

Acceptance: "I am at peace with all that has happened, is happening, and will happen."

Spiritual Awareness: "My nature is Divine; I am a spiritual being."

New Beginnings: "My life is just beginning."

Unique and Abundant: "I am unique, and my uniqueness is my greatest asset in making money."

Unique and Gifted: "I am unique, and my uniqueness is my gift to the world."

Double Gratitude: "I am deeply thankful for the abundance, the joy, and the love that surrounds me every day."

Self-Sufficiency: "All I need is within me now."

Authenticity: "I am authentic, powerful, and dynamic."

Focus and Efficiency: "I am focused, industrious, organized, and efficient."

Wisdom: "I am a genius, and I apply my wisdom."

Attraction: "My thoughts, my words, and my actions are

powerful forces of attraction."

Goal Achievement: "I always achieve my goals."

Radiance and Transformation: "I am brilliant, I am bright. I am a radiant being of light. I'm an outstanding peak performer. I'm a dynamic life transformer."

Repeat these affirmations daily, either in the morning to start your day with positivity or at night to reflect on your achievements. As you consistently reinforce these statements, they become a part of your mindset, guiding your thoughts, actions, and ultimately, your reality.

6. Daily "Weeding" of Negative Thoughts: Nurturing Your Mental Garden

Imagine your mind as a garden where your thoughts are the seeds. Just as you carefully tend to your garden to prevent weeds from taking over, you must do the same with your thoughts. Negative thoughts are like weeds; if left unchecked, they can choke out the positivity you're trying to cultivate.

The techniques introduced earlier in this journey are your gardening tools for dealing with these mental weeds. Let's explore how to use them effectively:

Cutting Off Negativity: When you notice a negative thought sprouting, cut it off. Replace it with a more positive and constructive thought. For example, if you catch yourself thinking, "I'll never succeed," cut it off and replace it with, "I am capable of achieving my goals."

Labelling Negative Thoughts: Identify negative thoughts for what they are – just thoughts. Label them as unhelpful or inaccurate. This helps you detach from their power over you. When you think, "I'm a failure," label it as a negative thought and remind yourself of your past successes.

Exaggeration to Absurdity: If a negative thought creeps in, exaggerate it to the point of absurdity. For instance, if you think, "I'm terrible at this," exaggerate it: "I'm the worst person in the world at this, and the universe is collapsing because of it." This technique helps you see the irrationality of such thoughts.

Counteraction with Positivity: Replace negative thoughts with their positive counterparts. If you find yourself thinking, "I'm unlovable," counteract it with, "I am worthy of love and affection." Your mind can only focus on one thought at a time; make it a positive one.

Remember, the key to maintaining a thriving mental garden is consistency. Daily "weeding" ensures that negative thoughts don't take root and undermine your progress. Just as you nurture your garden for a bountiful harvest, tend to your thoughts with care to reap the fruits of positivity in your life.

Random Acts of Kindness: Spreading the Seeds of Positivity

Kindness is a universal language that transcends boundaries. It's a powerful way to nurture positivity, both within yourself and in the world around you. Engaging in random acts of kindness is like sowing seeds of goodwill that can sprout into beautiful, positive experiences.

Here's how you can embrace this practice:

Simple Gestures: Acts of kindness don't have to be grand or costly. Simple gestures like holding the door for someone, offering a genuine compliment, or helping a neighbour with groceries can brighten someone's day.

Anonymous Giving: You can spread positivity anonymously. Leave a surprise note of encouragement for a coworker, pay for a stranger's coffee, or donate to a charity without seeking recognition.

Volunteer: Dedicate your time and energy to volunteer work. It could be at a local shelter, a community event, or any cause that resonates with you. Your efforts will not only benefit others but also fill your heart with fulfilment.

Listen Actively: Sometimes, the most significant act of kindness is simply listening. Be present when someone needs to talk, without judgment or interruption. Your empathy and understanding can make a world of difference.

Help in Times of Need: Offer your assistance when you notice someone struggling. It could be helping a friend move, offering a ride to someone without transportation, or cooking a meal for a family in need.

Spread Positivity Online: In today's digital age, you can spread kindness online too. Leave positive comments, share inspirational stories, or send uplifting messages to friends and acquaintances.

The beauty of random acts of kindness is that they create a ripple effect. Your kindness inspires others to pay it forward, creating a chain reaction of positivity. It also nourishes your own sense of well-being, as the act of giving brings joy and satisfaction.

So, make kindness a daily habit. It not only nurtures positivity within you but also contributes to creating a more compassionate and harmonious world for everyone.

End Your Day with Acknowledgment: Crafting Your Victory List

As you conclude your day, it's essential to take a moment for reflection and acknowledgement. This practice is like putting the final brushstroke on the canvas of your daily thoughts. It helps you appreciate your progress and nurture a positive mindset.

Here's how to make a Victory List:

Find a Quiet Space: Choose a peaceful and comfortable place where you won't be disturbed.

Relax Your Mind: Take a few deep breaths to calm your mind and body. Let go of any tension or stress.

Reflect on Your Day: Think about the events, experiences, and interactions you had during the day. What went well? What challenges did you overcome? What moments brought you joy or satisfaction?

List Your Victories: Start jotting down your victories. These can be both big and small accomplishments, moments of gratitude, or acts of kindness you received or gave. The key is to focus on the positive aspects of your day.

Express Gratitude: Alongside your victories, express gratitude for the good things that happened. Acknowledge the people, opportunities, or circumstances that made your day better.

Feel the Emotions: As you recall your victories and express gratitude, allow yourself to feel the emotions associated with them. Relive those moments of joy, achievement, or connection.

Visualize Success: As you complete your Victory List, take a moment to visualize the positive impact of these victories on your life. See how they contribute to your personal growth, happiness, and well-being.

Creating a Victory List serves multiple purposes:

Boosts Positivity: It shifts your focus from what didn't go well to what you accomplished and appreciated during the day.

Strengthens Resilience: Recognizing your victories reminds you of your ability to overcome challenges and make progress.

Fosters Gratitude: Expressing gratitude for the good things in your life enhances your overall sense of well-being.

Promotes Mindfulness: The process of reflection and acknowledgement keeps you grounded and present.

Sets a Positive Tone: Ending your day on a positive note can lead to more restful sleep and a better start to the next day.

Remember that your Victory List is personal to you. It reflects your unique experiences and perspective. Over time, this practice can become a powerful habit that helps you maintain a positive mindset, even in the face of challenges.

So, as you close the chapter on each day, craft your Victory List with intention and gratitude. Let it be a testament to your growth, resilience, and the positivity you're nurturing in your life.

The Power of Repetition: Building Thought Mastery

The saying, "Practice makes perfect," holds true when it comes to harnessing the power of your mind. The rituals and habits you've learned are most effective when you incorporate them into your daily routine consistently. This repetition is where the real magic happens. The key is persistent consistency.

Why Repetition Matters:

Reinforcing Neural Pathways: When you repeat positive practices like gratitude, affirmations, and weeding out negativity, you're essentially strengthening the neural pathways in your brain. It's like carving a groove in a well-worn path. The more you travel that path, the easier it becomes to follow.

Creating Lasting Habits: Repetition transforms actions into habits. Daily engagement with these practices makes them an integral part of your life. They become second nature, something you do automatically without thinking.

Deepening Mindfulness: Consistency fosters mindfulness. You become more aware of your thoughts, emotions, and intentions throughout the day. This heightened awareness empowers you to make intentional choices, rather than reacting impulsively.

Enhancing Positivity: Regularly engaging in positive practices reinforces a positive mindset. It shifts your default mental state from one of doubt or negativity to one of optimism and resilience.

Daily Commitment:

Imagine these practices as daily exercises for your mind. Just as you wouldn't expect to build physical strength with a single workout, mental mastery requires ongoing effort. Here's how to make repetition work for you:

Morning Ritual: Start your day with a routine that includes gratitude, setting intentions, contemplation, seeding, and visualization. These morning practices set a positive tone for the day ahead.

Throughout the Day: Be mindful of your thoughts and emotions. When negativity arises, use the techniques you've learned to counteract it immediately. This ongoing vigilance prevents negativity from taking root.

Evening Reflection: Before bed, craft your Victory List and reflect on your daily experiences. This helps you acknowledge your progress and maintain a positive mindset as you drift into sleep.

Consistency is Key: Consistency is more important than intensity. Even if you can only dedicate a few minutes to each practice, do them daily. Over time, you'll notice the cumulative effect of these habits.

Adapt and Evolve: As you progress on your journey of thought mastery, feel free to adapt these practices to suit your evolving needs and goals. Your mind is a dynamic landscape, and your routines can evolve with it.

Remember, there's no rush or finish line in the pursuit of thought mastery. It's a lifelong journey, and the true power lies in the dedication to daily repetition. With each day, you refine your ability to shape your reality, fostering a life filled with positivity, growth, and fulfilment.

Chapter 12:
Unveiling the Power Within: The Subconscious Mind and Beyond

All of us have our own inner fears, beliefs, and opinions. These inner assumptions rule and govern our lives. A suggestion has no power in and of itself, its power arises from the fact that you accept it mentally. As you sow in your subconscious mind, so shall you reap in your body and environment.

- Dr Joseph Murphy

In the intricate landscape of the human mind, the subconscious realm holds profound influence over our thoughts, actions, and the unfolding of our lives. This chapter delves into the depths of the subconscious, revealing its workings, the remarkable Reticular Activating System (RAS), the enigmatic realm of intuition, and how to tap into these hidden forces to harness your true potential.

The Subconscious Mind: A Hidden Powerhouse

The subconscious mind is like the vast, hidden expanse beneath the surface of an iceberg, where about 90% of its mass resides beneath the waterline. Here's a closer look at the workings of this enigmatic part of your psyche:

Storage of Experiences: Your subconscious is a reservoir that stores memories, experiences, and beliefs, both positive and negative, accumulated throughout your life. These experiences shape your perceptions, attitudes, and responses to various situations.

Automatic Functions: It is the source of your automatic functions, such as breathing, heart rate, and bodily sensations. It also governs your habits and routines, simplifying repetitive tasks.

Emotion and Imagination: The subconscious is the realm of emotions and imagination. It is the fertile soil where emotions take root and creative ideas flourish.

Belief System: Your belief system, which profoundly impacts your decisions and actions, resides here. Beliefs held in the subconscious often operate without conscious awareness.

The Reticular Activating System (RAS): Your Mind's Filtering Mechanism

Imagine the Reticular Activating System (RAS) as the

gatekeeper of your conscious mind. This neural network, located at the base of your brain, filters the overwhelming amount of information bombarding your senses, allowing only select stimuli to reach your conscious awareness. Here's how it works:

Selective Awareness: The RAS filters information based on your current priorities and goals. It directs your attention to what aligns with your intentions, effectively tuning out distractions.

Confirmation Bias: It actively seeks information that confirms your existing beliefs. This is why, when you focus on a specific goal, you suddenly notice relevant opportunities and resources seemingly everywhere.

Positive and Negative Feedback Loops: The RAS responds to your emotional states. If you consistently focus on negative thoughts, it can perpetuate negativity. Conversely, by maintaining a positive outlook, you invite more positivity into your life.

Meet Tom, an ordinary guy with an extraordinary goal, to buy his dream car, a sleek and rare sports car that he had admired for years. It wasn't just any car; it was the embodiment of his aspirations and symbolized his journey toward success.

Tom's decision to purchase this car marked a significant turning point in his life. Before, he had never paid much attention to this particular car model on the road. But now, as he set his sights on owning one, something incredible began to happen.

One day, Tom was driving to work, and he noticed the exact car he wanted parked at a nearby dealership. It was as if the car had suddenly materialized before him, even though it had always been there. Intrigued, he decided to visit the dealership after work to learn more about it.

As he walked into the showroom, he couldn't help but notice how prominently the car was displayed. The salesperson greeted him warmly and began to share all the incredible features and benefits of the car. Tom felt a sense of excitement and possibility building within him.

Over the next few weeks, Tom's awareness of this car model expanded. He started seeing it in advertisements, on the streets, and even in movies he watched. It was as though the car had become a part of his daily life. He also began to notice friends and acquaintances who owned this car, and they shared their experiences and insights with him.

Tom was doing more than just looking for this car; he was actively seeking information about it. He researched its specifications, read reviews, and joined online forums dedicated to enthusiasts of this particular vehicle. Conversations about this car became a regular part of his life.

With his newfound knowledge and focus, Tom set a clear goal to save for and ultimately purchase this car. He created a vision board adorned with pictures of the car and placed it prominently in his home office. Every day, he would spend a few minutes visualizing himself behind the wheel, feeling the leather seats, and hearing the roar of the engine.

Tom's journey to owning his dream car was not without its challenges. He had to work diligently to save money, make financial adjustments, and stay disciplined. Yet, he remained persistent because his goal had become crystal clear in his mind.

One day, after months of dedicated effort, Tom finally drove off the dealership lot in the car of his dreams. It was a moment of triumph, and he felt an overwhelming sense of accomplishment.

What happened in Tom's story was a manifestation of the

Reticular Activating System at work. When he decided that owning this car was a priority, his RAS went into action. It filtered through the vast amount of information in the world and brought to his attention everything related to that car. It became the focal point of his daily life, leading him to the resources, opportunities, and insights needed to make his dream a reality.

Tom's journey is a testament to the power of setting clear intentions and activating your Reticular Activating System. When you define what's important to you and remain focused on it, you begin to notice opportunities and resources that were always there but had previously gone unnoticed. Just like Tom, you can make your dreams come true by harnessing the incredible potential of your RAS.

The relationship between the conscious mind and the subconscious mind

The conscious mind is your computer, responsible for logic, reasoning, and decision making. It's the part of your mind that you actively control, like operating a computer program.

On the other hand, the subconscious mind is like the vast internet, immensely powerful and operating silently beneath the surface. It's responsible for storing your beliefs, values, self-confidence, habits, and emotions. These aspects of your psyche often run on autopilot, shaping your thoughts, behaviours, and responses without your conscious awareness.

Let's delve a bit deeper into this analogy:

Conscious Mind (The Computer):

Willpower: Think of willpower as your ability to consciously make decisions and choices. It's like manually selecting which websites to visit on the internet. You can use your willpower to decide your actions consciously.

Analytical Processes: Just as a computer processes data logically, your conscious mind handles analytical thinking, problem-solving, and critical reasoning. It dissects information logically and draws conclusions.

Decision Making: Your conscious mind is where you weigh options and make choices. It's like actively selecting and executing commands on a computer.

Subconscious Mind (The Internet):

Beliefs: Your beliefs are deeply ingrained in your subconscious. They're like web pages scattered throughout the internet. These beliefs can significantly influence your conscious decisions and actions without you realizing it.

Values: Your values act as the underlying principles guiding your life, much like the foundational infrastructure of the internet. They shape your priorities and what you find meaningful.

Self-Confidence: Self-confidence is a subconscious attribute. It's like the underlying programming code of websites, determining how they function. Your self-confidence, or lack thereof, influences how you approach various aspects of life.

Habits: Habits are like well-established websites on the internet. They are automatic routines stored in your subconscious. These habits can either propel you toward your goals or hinder your progress.

Emotions: Emotions are the responses and interactions you have with the internet's content. They can be influenced by the information stored in your subconscious. Positive emotions can be linked to positive beliefs and experiences, while negative emotions may stem from negative beliefs and memories.

Understanding this analogy helps you recognize the vast influence of your subconscious mind. It operates silently in the background, shaping your thoughts, behaviours, and experiences. To make lasting changes in your life, it's essential to explore and reprogram your subconscious, just as you might fine-tune your internet usage to find more valuable and positive content. Through techniques like affirmations, visualization, and meditation, you can access and rewire your subconscious to align with your conscious goals and desires.

Intuition: Navigating the Subconscious Realm

Intuition is your innate ability to tap into the vast knowledge stored in your subconscious. It's that gut feeling, inner knowing, or sudden insight that often defies logic. Here's how to harness your intuition:

Meditation and Mindfulness: These practices quiet the conscious mind's chatter, allowing intuitive insights to surface.

Journaling: Maintain a journal to record your intuitive hunches and experiences. Over time, patterns may emerge.

Trust Your Gut: Learn to trust your intuition. Sometimes, it's that subtle inner nudge guiding you in the right direction.

Silence and Solitude: Spend time in solitude to connect with your inner wisdom. Intuitive insights often emerge in quiet moments.

The Iceberg Analogy

Consider your conscious mind as the visible tip of the iceberg, floating above the water. It's aware, analytical, and limited in its scope. However, beneath the surface lies the vast subconscious, akin to the submerged bulk of the iceberg. Here, your true power resides, in influencing your thoughts, decisions, and experiences.

Tapping into the Subconscious: Practical Exercises

Affirmations: Program your subconscious with positive affirmations to instil new beliefs and thought patterns.

Visualization: Use vivid mental imagery to communicate with your subconscious. Visualize your goals and desires as already achieved.

Journaling: Record your dreams and analyse recurring themes or symbols for insights into your subconscious processes.

Your subconscious mind operates like an expansive network, processing information and emotions in ways that often elude our conscious awareness. One powerful avenue of communication with this hidden realm is through your dreams.

Setting the Stage:

Affirmation Before Sleep: Before drifting into slumber, recite a simple affirmation: "Tonight, I will dream, and I will remember my dreams." Repetition is key; this primes your subconscious to engage with you during the night.

Dream Journal: Keep a dedicated dream journal by your bedside. As soon as you wake, jot down every detail you recall from your dreams. Don't fret if the memories appear fragmented; even small fragments can offer valuable insights.

Deciphering the Language:

Emotions: Start your interpretation by examining the emotions that your dreams stirred within you. Were you happy, anxious, or excited? These dream emotions often mirror your subconscious feelings about your waking life.

Symbols and Patterns: Pay attention to recurring symbols, themes, or patterns in your dreams. These symbols may carry personal meanings or broader cultural significance. Your subconscious employs these symbols to convey ideas and emotions indirectly.

Personal Relevance: Consider how your dream relates to your current life circumstances or challenges. Dreams sometimes unveil creative solutions or provide fresh perspectives on real-life issues.

Internal Dialogue: Engage in a form of self-reflection where you mentally revisit your dream. Step back into the dream's setting and converse with its characters or symbols. Pose questions and observe the responses or insights that emerge.

By consistently practising these techniques and attentively observing your dreams, you can forge a deeper connection with your subconscious mind. Over time, this connection can lead to heightened self-awareness, personal growth, and the capacity to tap into your subconscious wisdom for effective problem-solving and informed decision-making in your waking life.

The subconscious mind is a profound well of untapped potential. Understanding its workings, along with the influence of the Reticular Activating System and intuition, can empower you to navigate life with greater awareness and purpose. Like the hidden bulk of the iceberg, your subconscious holds the key to transforming your reality and harnessing the full extent of your mind's power.

Chapter 13: The Subconscious Healer:
Unleashing the Power of the Mind for Health

Trust the subconscious mind to heal you. It made your body, and it knows all of its processes and functions. It knows much more than your conscious mind about healing and restoring you to perfect balance.

- Dr Joseph Murphy

In the grand symphony of your existence, your subconscious mind plays a pivotal role in orchestrating your health and well-being. Beyond its influence on thoughts, habits, and behaviours, your subconscious mind possesses a remarkable ability to influence your physical health, often in ways that defy conventional explanations. This chapter delves into the mysterious and potent realm of the subconscious mind as it relates to health and explores the intriguing phenomenon of the placebo effect.

The Hidden Powerhouse:

Hidden beneath the surface of your conscious awareness lies the subconscious mind, a vast reservoir of untapped potential. In matters of health, this hidden powerhouse can be your greatest ally or unwitting saboteur. Understanding its influence is key to harnessing its potential.

The Subconscious Blueprint:

Consider your subconscious mind as the architect of your body. It stores every piece of information about your physical health, from your cellular functions to your immune responses. Like a diligent librarian, it keeps a record of your body's history, including your past illnesses, injuries, and genetic predispositions.

The Placebo Effect: A Glimpse into the Subconscious:

One of the most compelling illustrations of the subconscious mind's power is the placebo effect. When a person experiences genuine improvements in health after receiving a treatment with no active ingredients (a placebo), it underscores the mind's influence on the body.

How the Placebo Effect Works:

The placebo effect operates through a complex interplay of psychological and neurological mechanisms. When someone believes in the effectiveness of a treatment, their subconscious mind interprets this belief as a directive to initiate physical changes.

The Brain's Response:

Remarkably, the brain releases neurotransmitters and endorphins in response to this belief. These natural chemicals can reduce pain, boost mood, and even enhance the body's ability to heal. In essence, the subconscious mind can trigger a physiological response simply through the power of belief.

Mind Over Matter:

While the placebo effect has been well-documented, the broader implication is profound: our subconscious beliefs and expectations can significantly impact our health. This implies that your mind can be a potent tool for self-healing.

Harnessing Subconscious Healing:

Mindful Belief: Be mindful of your beliefs about health and healing. Cultivate a positive and optimistic mindset, as your subconscious will interpret this as an instruction for well-being.

Visualization: Engage in healing visualizations. Imagine your body in perfect health, with every cell functioning optimally. Visualize your immune system as an army of protectors, guarding your well being

Affirmations: Use affirmations tailored to health and healing. Phrases like "My body is a temple of health" and "Every day, I am getting healthier and stronger" can resonate with your subconscious mind.

Placebo's Lesson: Recognize the power of belief and the placebo effect. Understand that your mind has the ability to influence your body's responses and leverage this knowledge for your benefit.

The Subconscious Healer in Everyday Life:

Beyond the placebo effect, your subconscious mind continually contributes to your health in more subtle ways. It governs your habits, which can either promote or undermine wellness. Understanding how your subconscious mind operates can empower you to make healthier choices, from diet and exercise to stress management and sleep.

The Journey Ahead:

As you embark on a journey to unlock the healing potential of your subconscious mind, remember that it's a dynamic process. Regular practice, positive reinforcement, and self-awareness are your allies. By aligning your conscious intent with the hidden wisdom of your subconscious, you open the door to a realm of health and vitality you may never have fully explored before.

In the realm of health, your subconscious mind is a silent but powerful partner. By nurturing this partnership and working in harmony with your subconscious, you can cultivate a state of well-being that extends far beyond the physical, embracing the holistic nature of health that encompasses mind, body, and spirit.

Dr Carl Simonton was a pioneer in the field of psycho-oncology, which explores the psychological and emotional aspects of cancer care. He is best known for his work in using visualization and guided imagery techniques to help cancer patients cope with their illness and improve their quality of life. Here is an overview of Dr Carl Simonton's approach:

Mind-Body Connection: Dr Simonton believed in the strong connection between the mind and the body. He argued that a patient's mental and emotional state could significantly impact their physical health and the course of their illness.

Visualization: One of his primary techniques involved guided imagery and visualization. He encouraged patients to use their imagination to create mental images of their immune system attacking and destroying cancer cells. This process aimed to strengthen the patient's belief in their body's ability to fight the disease.

Positive Affirmations: Dr Simonton also encouraged the use of positive affirmations. Patients were encouraged to repeat positive statements about their health and recovery to reinforce a positive mindset.

Stress Reduction: Stress reduction techniques, such as relaxation exercises, meditation, and deep breathing, were integral to his approach. Lowering stress levels was seen as vital to supporting the immune system and overall well-being.

Patient Empowerment: Simonton's approach emphasized empowering patients to take an active role in their healing process. By visualizing positive outcomes and maintaining a positive mindset, patients could feel more in control of their health.

Supportive Care: Importantly, Dr Simonton's techniques were typically used as complementary strategies alongside conventional cancer treatments, not as standalone replacements. He believed that a holistic approach that included both medical treatment and psychological support was essential.

Scientific Studies: While some patients reported positive outcomes from using these techniques, it's important to note that the scientific evidence supporting their effectiveness in curing cancer is limited. However, many patients found these practices beneficial in reducing stress, improving their mental outlook, and enhancing their overall quality of life.

Dr Carl Simonton's work has influenced the field of psychosocial oncology and integrative cancer care, recognizing the importance of addressing the emotional and psychological needs of cancer patients alongside medical treatment. It's important for individuals with cancer to discuss any complementary therapies with their healthcare team to ensure they are safe and appropriate for their specific situation.

Chapter 14: Unleashing Your Potential:
The Power of Self-Image

You cannot consistently perform in a manner which is inconsistent with the way you see yourself.

- Dr Joyce Brothers

In the grand tapestry of personal mastery, few threads are as vital as the concept of self-image. It is the intricate mosaic of beliefs, perceptions, and thoughts that we hold about ourselves. This chapter delves into the profound role of self-image in shaping our reality, expanding our limitations, and celebrating the unique individuals we are.

The Two Stories We Tell Ourselves:

Every person has two stories that narrate their existence. The first is the story of their life, unique to them alone, filled with experiences, memories, and moments that define their journey. But it's the second story, the one they tell themselves every day, that often holds the most sway. This internal narrative, shaped by our self-image, is the lens through which we perceive the world and ourselves within it.

The Self-Imposed Box:

Imagine your self-image as a box, a comfortable yet confining space that defines who you believe you are. This box, created by the thoughts and beliefs you hold about yourself, can either limit your potential or serve as a launching pad for greatness. The boundaries of this box determine how far you're willing to reach and what heights you dare to scale.

The Consistency Principle:

Here's a profound truth: You will always act in alignment with your self-image. If you see yourself as unworthy of success, you will subconsciously sabotage opportunities for achievement. Conversely, if you perceive yourself as capable and deserving, you'll instinctively strive for excellence.

Expanding the Self-Image:

The good news is that your self-image isn't a fixed reality; it's an artificial construct held together by your thoughts. You possess the power to expand it, to redraw its boundaries, and in doing so, to transform yourself. By reshaping your self-image, you shatter the constraints that limit your potential.

Embracing Your Uniqueness:

You are a marvel of creation, a one-of-a-kind masterpiece. In a world of nearly 8 billion people, there is no one else quite like you. It's not merely a matter of recognizing your individuality; it's about boldly proclaiming it. Embrace your uniqueness as a precious gift that you bring to the world.

I am enough.

I am positive, I love with my whole heart.

I am fiercely loyal and beautifully vulnerable.

I am independent, strong and courageous.

I am compassionate and creative.

I am authentic with my words and my sentiments.

I practice kindness and I forgive easily.

I make mistakes – but I learn from them.

I am ecstatic when my friends succeed.

I take risks because my faith is stronger than my fear.

I never apologize for who I am.

Every day in every way I am a better version of myself.

I am synchronous.

I am enough.

In the grand tapestry of personal mastery, this chapter on self-image is a testament to the power of belief and self-love. It's a reminder that we are the artists of our own existence, capable of crafting a self-image that propels us toward our highest aspirations. With each stroke of self-affirmation, we step into the boundless potential of who we truly are.

Chapter 15: It Starts with Everything: The Power of Habit Transformation

Sow a thought, and you reap an act; Sow an act, and you reap a habit; Sow a habit, and you reap a character; Sow a character, and you reap a destiny.

- Ralph Waldo Emerson

In this chapter, we bring the journey of personal mastery full circle. Throughout this guide, you've gained insights into harnessing the incredible potential of your mind, the significance of self-image, and the art of thought mastery. Now, we arrive at a pivotal juncture where it all begins: the transformation of your habits.

The Mind's Energy Reservoir:

Your ability to create lasting change in your life hinges on the energy reserves of your mind. While the mind is a powerful tool, it operates within constraints. We've asked you to embrace responsibilities, conquer fears, practice discipline, and maintain motivation – endeavours that demand considerable mental energy.

Consider this: if you have only a few precious hours outside of work to pursue your aspirations, the struggle becomes real. The challenge escalates when you're grappling with stress and burnout. To unlock your fullest potential, you must turn the spotlight inward and focus on rejuvenating your mental and physical energy.

Starting with Small Shifts:

Transformation begins with small, manageable steps. To optimize your mental energy, begin with the basics. Ensure you're getting sufficient sleep, savour moments in the sun, and consider dietary supplements that support your well-being. These foundational changes pave the way for more profound shifts.

From Basic to Profound Transformation:

As you build your energy reserves, delve into deeper aspects of self-improvement. Cultivate the art of meditation to centre your mind. Discover your passions and surround yourself with like-minded individuals who inspire and uplift you. Each facet of your health and lifestyle feeds into your emotional and mental well-being, amplifying your potential.

The Attitude of Gratitude:

The ultimate key to happiness lies in the attitude of gratitude. It's natural to aspire to better circumstances, but dwelling in perpetual longing can lead to dissatisfaction. The hedonistic treadmill keeps you in a perpetual cycle of pursuit. Instead, pause and appreciate the blessings you already possess.

Focus on the Here and Now:

Embrace the present moment. You don't need a widescreen TV, a vacation, or a job change to find contentment. Begin today, recognizing the value in your current circumstances. Shift your perspective to a "gratitude mindset," and you'll discover an abundance of happiness in your daily life.

Chapter 16: Conclusion:
Your Journey to Personal Mastery

Discipline comes through self-control. This means that you must control all negative qualities. Before you can control conditions, you must first control yourself. Self-mastery is the hardest job you will ever tackle. If you do not conquer self, you will be conquered by self.

- Napoleon Hill

As we conclude this guide, remember that personal mastery is a continuous journey, not a final destination. Your mind is a canvas, and your life is a masterpiece in the making. Start small, transform your habits, and watch as your life undergoes remarkable changes. You don't have to be great to begin, but you must begin to become great. It starts with everything, and it starts with you.

So, as you embark on your path of personal mastery, remember: You are enough, and your journey is uniquely yours. Embrace it with gratitude, and let your inner light shine brightly for the world to see.

Live in those moments.

> *You can have everything in life you want if you will just help enough other people get what they want,*
>
> - Zig Ziglar

I have lived by this quote for most of my life, legacy only happens when you help other people be, do and have more than they thought was possible. The purpose of life is to help others, if you can't help them you are not supposed to hurt them. Always treat people by applying the golden rule. Treat other people as you would like to be treated. Always be courteous and sincere, and be true to yourself. Remember that you mine people like you mine gold, no one runs into a gold mine looking for dirt, but you have to go through a lot of dirt to get to the gold. Be a good finder, always look for the good in everything. Life is a journey where each day is a gift that is why it is called the present. Stop living in the past you can't change it, stop living in the future tomorrow is promised to no one, start living in the present that is all you have. You have one life make it count. Remember nothing starts until you do. You don't have to be great to start but you have to start, to be great. It starts with deciding what you are after, and what you want from life. Until you decide until you take action nothing will change.

You are what you are and where you are because of what has gone into your mind. You can change where you are and what you are by changing what goes into your mind. Zig Ziglar stated that what you feed your mind determines your appetite. There is great power in becoming influenced by the things you read, watch and listen to. That is why it is so important to feed your mind with the right positive stuff.

5 Steps to a great day: Steyn Rossouw

1. I believe our day is determined by the way we get up in the morning. Do you get up and say good god it is morning, or do you get up and say Good Morning God. Bob Baudine talks about two chairs. You should always start your day with two chairs, one for you and one for God. You are allowed to have a deep and insightful conversation with God every day. When you are challenged always remember these three questions.

a) Does God know about your problems?

b) Does He have a plan for them?

c) Are they too big for Him?

I believe starting this way will change your life

2. Everyone has a story and the most important story is the one you tell yourself. I believe you should have a chat with yourself every morning before your day starts. This is the time to look at yourself in the mirror and say, "Good golly I like you!!" It is the time to acknowledge yourself and to be thankful. You see if you do not like who you are, if you do not trust who and what you are if you have no confidence in yourself how can you expect anyone else to believe in you, to trust and like you? It starts with you first.

3. The third thing I want you to do every morning, is to go into your bathroom, put your head between your hands and for five minutes flat, WORRY, worry about each and everything you can find to worry about. I know we all worry about stuff, but here is the truth, in 57 years I have not met or found one person who could tell me, Steyn I worried about this and then it changed. I worried about my finances and it filled my bank. I worried about my business and my profits went through the roof. Worrying does not change anything taking action does. So, worry early in the morning and then close the bathroom door on the worries and start making a difference.

4. Acknowledge every day as a gift and that the purpose of life is to help others. It is not about being able to help millions of people. We often think we cannot make a difference. I always remember the Tale of the Starfish: Once upon a time, on a sprawling beach where the waves kissed the shore, a man encountered a young boy. The boy was meticulously picking up stranded starfish, one by one, and tossing them back into the ocean. The man, intrigued and perhaps perplexed, approached the boy to inquire about his purpose.

With a warm smile, the boy explained his mission. The tide was receding, and the surf was growing stronger. Without intervention, the stranded starfish would succumb to the relentless sun and eventually perish. The boy's actions aimed to give these helpless creatures a fighting chance at survival.

The man, his curiosity piqued, questioned the boy's endeavour. He pointed out the vastness of the beach, the multitude of starfish strewn across it, and the futility, as it seemed, of one person's efforts. "Surely," he mused, "you can't make a difference amidst this endless expanse of starfish and beach."

The boy, undeterred by scepticism, continued his task. He bent down, picked up a stranded starfish, and tenderly returned it to the ocean's embrace. With a smile that radiated compassion, he turned to the man and said, "I made a difference for that one."

The starfish story offers a profound lesson – that the magnitude of impact is not solely measured by the number of lives touched but by the sincerity of intent and the depth of care invested in each action. It reminds us that even in the face of overwhelming challenges, taking action, no matter how modest is a beacon of hope. Each time the boy rescued a starfish, he triggered a ripple of change. He symbolized the power of kindness, demonstrating that even small acts can set in motion waves of positivity that extend far beyond their immediate effect. The starfish story invites us to embrace a similar outlook in our own lives. It reminds us that no matter how vast the problems we encounter may seem, every act of kindness, every gesture of compassion, and every effort to make a positive difference is meaningful. Each one of us carries the potential to be the boy in the story, to reach out and touch the lives of others. We may not be able to change the entire world, but we can change someone's world. Whether it's through a kind word, a helping hand, or a simple act of generosity, we have the capacity to create a ripple of positivity.

As we journey through life, let us remember the starfish story as a guiding light. May it inspire us to be compassionate, to take action, and to believe in the significance of our efforts. In doing so, we become beacons of hope, making a difference, one life at a time.

In life, we often forget how big a difference we can make to one person at a time. Always be kind and courteous and perform a random act of kindness every day.

5. Take stock every day. Before you go to sleep look back at your day and ask yourself, did I today live my life to the fullest, did I make a difference for one person, did I work on my goals, did I achieve what I set out to achieve this day? If the answer to these questions is yes, may you have a good sleep and rest, and may your life be abundantly blessed.

Allow me to close this book by acknowledging and saying a big thank you to each and every person who has made an impact on my life. To those whom I am not mentioning let me say thank you to you first.

To my dearest wife Celeste, you are my inspiration and my motivation for always wanting to be a better person, you have taught me what love, kindness and support mean, I love you. Thank you for always supporting me in everything I do.

To my parents for teaching me to be hardworking and honest and to try everything in life. To keep the good and to get rid of the bad. To do the good things twice.

To my children, Ricardo, Franshua and Marinique, for being a blessing and teaching me to be humble.

To my best friend Roland Cullinan for teaching me the true meaning of unconditional friendship.

To my mentors Zig Ziglar, Tom Ziglar, Julie Ziglar Norman Cindy Ziglar, Bob Beaudine, Howard Partridge, Dr Robert Rohm, Tom Hopkins, John Kehoe, Sir Andrew Newton, Tony Robbins and each and every other person I have encountered throughout my life, I have learned from all of you and I am truly grateful for each and every one of you for you have made a profound difference in my life.

30-Day Mind Mastery Challenge: Unleash Your Full Potential

It is not the critic who counts; not the man who points out how the strong man stumbles, or where the doer of deeds could have done them better. The credit belongs to the man who is actually in the arena, whose face is marred by dust and sweat and blood; who strives valiantly; who errs, who comes short again and again, because there is no effort without error and shortcoming; but who does actually strive to do the deeds; who knows great enthusiasms, the great devotions; who spends himself in a worthy cause; who at the best knows, in the end, the triumph of high achievement, and who at the worst, if he fails, at least fails while daring greatly, so that his place shall never be with those cold and timid souls who neither knows victory nor defeat.

- Theodore Roosevelt

30-Day Mind Mastery Challenge: Unleash Your Full Potential

Welcome to the 30-Day Mind Mastery Challenge! Over the next month, you will embark on a transformative journey to unlock the immense power of your mind. This challenge is designed to help you develop mental resilience, enhance your focus, and harness the incredible potential of your thoughts. Are you ready to take control of your mind and, in turn, your life? Let's get started!

Day 1: Set Your Intentions

Today, take a moment to reflect on your goals and aspirations.

Write down what you hope to achieve in the next 30 days.

Define your intentions clearly and vividly.

Do the Wheel of Life

Read each of the category lists carefully and rate yourself on a scale of 1-10 in each space.

Rate yourself with 1 being very poor and 10 being outstanding.

For example, under Physical, rate your own appearance. Do you look fit and well-kept?

Do this for all of the categories. You may have done this before. That's OK, you need to do it again and again - and every six months for the rest of your life.

Now add up the total of each column and divide that number by 10.

This will give you your personal score for that particular spoke on the wheel

PHYSICAL

Appearance

Regular checkup

Energy level

Muscles toned

Regular fitness program

Weight control

Diet and Nutrition

Stress control

Endurance and strength

Enough sleep

TOTAL ÷ 10 =

FINANCIAL

Proper priority

Personal budget

Impulse purchases

Earnings

Living within income

Money in savings

Adequate insurance

Investments

Financial statement

Debt free

TOTAL ÷ 10 =

SPIRITUAL

Believe in God

Inner peace

Influence on others

Spouse relationship

Church involvement

Sense of purpose

Attitude for giving donations

Prayer

Bible study

Abundant gratitude

TOTAL ÷ 10 =

PERSONAL

Recreation

Exercise

Friendships

Community activities

Service clubs

Quiet time

Growth time

Consistent life

Appropriate social media

Time management

TOTAL ÷ 10 =

MENTAL

Attitude

Intelligence

Formal education

Continuing education & training

Creative imagination

Inspirational reading

Inquisitive mind

Self-image

Enthusiasm

Automobile university *

TOTAL ÷ 10 =

CAREER

Love what I do

Understand my job

Co-worker relationships

Productivity

Understand company goals

Understand my activity in relation to my goals

Appreciate company benefits

Opportunity for advancement

Well-trained for my job

Own my business/have a career path

TOTAL ÷ 10 =

FAMILY

Listening

Good role model

Principled but flexible

Forgiving attitude

Build the self-esteem of others

Express love and respect

Meals together

Family relationships

Dealing with disagreements

Time together

TOTAL ÷ 10 =

* Zig Ziglar popularized the concept of Automobile University–the concept of using the time in your car to listen to educational lectures.

Day 2: Goal Setting Process

Set specific goals for each area, writing down what you want to do, be, and have.

For each goal, ask "why" until you find a deep and meaningful reason. If you can't find a compelling "why" in one sentence, consider removing it from your list.

Apply the following steps to each goal:

- Identify the goal.
- Determine the benefits of reaching the goal.
- Explore the obstacles and reasons why you haven't achieved it yet.
- List the skills and knowledge needed.
- Identify who you need to collaborate with.
- Create a detailed action plan.
- Set a deadline for achieving the goal.
- Set a goal for each spoke of the Wheel of Life.

What you get by achieving your goals is not as important as what you become by achieving your goals.

- Zig Ziglar

Day 3: Habit Change

Pick one spoke of the wheel.

Take action!

What bad habit do you have in this area?

What good habit will you replace the bad habit with?

Three Questions to Transformation

1. What are my desires, dreams, and goals for my mental life?

2. How will my life be better in the mental area when I achieve my mindset desires?

3. How can I apply grit to my gifts, talents, skills, and experience in the mental area of my life?

Use this process every day to replace one bad habit with one good habit.

> *The fastest way to success is to replace bad habits with good habits.*
>
> - Tom Ziglar

Day 4: Gratitude Journal

- Start a gratitude journal.
- Write down three things you're grateful for every morning
- Cultivate an attitude of appreciation.

Replace another bad habit with a good habit using the process from day 3.

> *Acknowledging the good that you already have in your life is the foundation for all abundance.*
>
> - Eckhardt Tolle

Day 5: Mind Work

Contemplate the following statement for 5 minutes:

"My mind is an amazing instrument of power that is transforming my life, now that I'm learning to use it".

Contemplate the following statement for 5 minutes:

"My personal vibration determines the circumstances and situations that happen to me. My thoughts and my beliefs create my personal vibration".

Self-observation: Several times every day, right in the midst of doing something, stop and catch yourself thinking. Observe your mind in action.

Weeding of negatives: Begin to weed out negatives by experimenting with the 4 techniques. (There is no time limit with this exercise.)

Replace another bad habit with a good habit.

Remember to do your gratitude journal every morning.

> *What you picture in your mind, your mind will go to work to accomplish. When you change your pictures, you automatically change your performance.*
>
> - Zig Ziglar

Day 6: Self-Reflection

Start your day with three things you are grateful for in your gratitude journal.

Replace another bad habit with a good habit.

Take this day to pause and reflect on your journey so far.

Review your Wheel of Life, goals, and habit changes.

Acknowledge any insights or progress you've made.

> *You attract what you are, not what you want. So if you want it then reflect it.*
>
> - Tony Gaskins

Day 7: Creating a Powerful Vision Board

Gather Supplies: Collect magazines, images, quotes, and materials that resonate with your goals and desires.

Clarify Your Goals: Before you start, be clear about your objectives. What do you want to achieve or manifest in your life?

Choose Your Base: Get a large poster board, corkboard, or digital platform (for a virtual vision board).

Select Images and Words: Go through your materials and choose images, words, and symbols that represent your goals and resonate with you emotionally.

Arrange and Glue: Arrange the chosen elements on your board in a visually appealing manner. Glue or attach them securely.

Visualize Success: Spend time each day looking at your vision board and visualizing the success, happiness, and fulfilment associated with your goals.

Feel the Emotions: As you gaze at your vision board, feel the emotions associated with achieving your goals as if they are happening right now.

Review Regularly: Regularly review and update your vision board as your goals evolve or you accomplish them.

Place It Strategically: Put your vision board in a location where you'll see it every day, like your bedroom or workspace.

Believe in Your Dreams: Maintain unwavering belief in your ability to manifest what's on your vision board.

Remember, your vision board is a powerful tool to reinforce your goals and keep your aspirations in focus. The more you engage with it, the more it can influence your thoughts and actions, leading you toward your desired future.

> *Be brave enough to live the life of your dreams according to your vision and purpose instead of the expectations and opinions of others.*
>
> - Roy T Bennett

Day 8: Visualization Exercise

Start your day with three things you are grateful for in your gratitude journal.

Replace another bad habit with a good habit.

Spend 15 minutes visualizing your goals.

Imagine achieving them in great detail.

Feel the emotions associated with your success.

Pick a quality or characteristic that you want to possess. Spend 5 minutes every day visualising yourself possessing that quality.

For 5 minutes every day, "seed" what it would feel like to have that quality.

The visions we cultivate within our minds shape the realities we live in; deliberately constructing these visions allows us to sculpt our future selves with purpose and intention.

- Steyn Rossouw

Day 9: Positive Affirmations

Start your day with three things you are grateful for in your gratitude journal.

Replace another bad habit with a good habit.

Create a list of positive affirmations.

Repeat them aloud in the morning and evening.

Boost your self-belief and confidence.

Watch your manner of speech if you wish to develop a peaceful state of mind. Start each day by affirming peaceful contented and happy attitudes and your days will tend to be pleasant and successful.

- Norman Vincent Peale

Day 10: What is holding you back?

Start your day with three things you are grateful for in your gratitude journal.

Replace another bad habit with a good habit.

Objective: Identify and break through limiting beliefs and fears that are holding you back from achieving your goals.

Instructions:

Self-Reflection: Find a quiet space where you won't be disturbed. Take a few deep breaths to calm your mind.

Identify Limiting Beliefs and Fears:

Write down a specific goal or aspiration you have.

Beneath it, jot down any beliefs or fears that come to mind that might be holding you back. These could be things like "I'm not good enough," "I'm too old," or "I'm too afraid of failure."

Question Your Beliefs:

For each belief or fear you've listed, ask yourself: "Is this belief/fear absolutely true?"

Challenge the validity of these beliefs. Are they based on facts, or are they assumptions or perceptions?

Seek Evidence to the Contrary:

For each belief or fear, try to recall instances in your life where it wasn't true or where you've overcome similar obstacles.

Write down this evidence next to each belief/fear.

Reframe Your Beliefs:

Rewrite each limiting belief into a positive, empowering statement. For example, change "I'm not good enough," to "I have the skills and potential to succeed."

Visualization:

Close your eyes and visualize yourself achieving your goal, now armed with these empowering beliefs. Feel the confidence and determination flowing through you.

Affirmations:

Create affirmations based on your empowering beliefs. Repeat these affirmations daily to reinforce your new mindset.

Action Plan:

Outline specific actions you can take to work towards your goal with your newfound beliefs and confidence.

Start with small, manageable steps that will build your momentum.

Accountability and Support:

Share your revised beliefs, affirmations, and action plan with a trusted friend, family member, or coach who can support and hold you accountable.

Daily Practice:

Commit to practising this exercise regularly, especially when you encounter moments of self-doubt or fear.

Monitor your progress and adjust your beliefs and actions as needed.

Breaking through limiting beliefs and fears is an ongoing process. By challenging and reframing these obstacles, you empower yourself to move forward with confidence and determination, ultimately achieving your goals.

The only person who is truly holding you back is you. No more excuses, it's time to change. It's time to live life at a new level.

\- Tony Robbins

Day 11: My Unique Life

Start your day with three things you are grateful for in your gratitude journal.

Replace another bad habit with a good habit.

Make a list of 50 qualities or attributes you believe you have, and write down everything you like about yourself.

You were designed for accomplishment, engineered for success, and endowed with the seeds of greatness.

- Zig Ziglar

Day 12: Daily Victory List - Celebrating Your Daily Wins

Start your day with three things you are grateful for in your gratitude journal.

Replace another bad habit with a good habit.

Make creating a Victory List a daily practice. Set aside a specific time, such as before bedtime, to reflect on your day and document your victories.

Consistency is key to reaping the full benefits of this exercise.

Reflect on Your Day:

Take a few moments to think about the events, experiences, and interactions you had during the day. What went well? What challenges did you overcome? What moments brought you joy or satisfaction?

1.   List Your Victories:

Start jotting down your victories. These can include accomplishments, acts of kindness, progress towards your goals, or any positive moments you experienced throughout the day.

Be specific. Instead of just writing "worked on a project," you could write "made significant progress on the project by completing the research phase."

2.   Express Gratitude:

Alongside your victories, express gratitude for the good things that happened. Acknowledge the people, opportunities, or circumstances that contributed to your successes.

Gratitude enhances your overall sense of well-being.

3.   Feel the Emotions:

As you recall your victories and express gratitude, allow yourself to feel the emotions associated with them. Relive those moments of joy, achievement, or connection.

4.   Visualize Success:

As you complete your Victory List, take a moment to visualize the positive impact of these victories on your life. See how they contribute to your personal growth, happiness, and well-being.

5.   Document Regularly:

Make creating a Victory List a daily practice. Set aside a specific time, such as before bedtime, to reflect on your day and document your victories.

Consistency is key to reaping the full benefits of this exercise.

6.   Be Specific and Honest:

Don't shy away from acknowledging even the smallest victories. Every positive experience counts.

Be honest with yourself; authenticity in your reflections is crucial.

7.   Use a Journal or Digital Tool:

You can keep a physical journal, or a digital document, or even use a dedicated app for creating your Victory List.

Whatever method you choose, make it convenient and accessible.

8.   Celebrate Your Wins:

Celebrate your victories, no matter how minor they may seem. Acknowledging and celebrating your successes boosts your self-esteem and motivation.

9.   Share with Others (Optional):

If you feel comfortable, you can share your Victory List with a friend, family member, or mentor. Sharing your wins can foster a sense of accountability and encouragement.

Creating a Victory List is a practice of positivity and self-appreciation. Over time, it helps you recognize your progress, build resilience, and maintain a positive mindset, even during challenging times.

> *Forgive yourself for not knowing what you didn't know until you lived through it. Honour your path. Trust your journey. Learn, grow, evolve, become.*
>
> - Creig Crippen

Day 13: Mindful Contemplation

Start your day with three things you are grateful for in your gratitude journal.

Replace another bad habit with a good habit.

Contemplation exercise:

Rewrite the six laws into the personal. For example: thoughts are real forces becomes my thoughts are real forces.

Spend 5 minutes every day contemplating the six laws.

Contemplate the following statement for several minutes every day:

My power to think thoughts is my power to create in my life.

I have the power to think whatever thoughts I choose.

Self-observation exercise:

Ask yourself several times during the course of the day:

How am I feeling? What am I thinking?

Weed out negatives by using techniques.

Close your day by adding three things to your victory list.

> *Mindful contemplation is the gentle whisper of the soul, weaving through the chaos of thought, to reveal the symphony of inner wisdom and peace within.*
>
> - Steyn Rossouw

Day 14: Random Act of Kindness

Start your day with three things you are grateful for in your gratitude journal.

Replace another bad habit with a good habit.

Perform a random act of kindness for someone.

It could be a small gesture or a significant favour.

Experience the joy of giving without expecting anything in return.

Performing a random act of kindness should be a daily practice.

Journal your thoughts.

Spend time journaling your thoughts and emotions.

Reflect on your experiences and insights.

Gain clarity and self-awareness.

Close your day by adding three things to your victory list.

> *Too often we underestimate the power of a touch a smile a kind word a listening ear an honest compliment or the smallest of caring all of which have the potential to turn a life around.*
>
> - Leo Buscaglia

Day 15: Learn Something New

Congratulations on reaching Day 15 of the 30-day challenge! As the creator of this challenge, I want to acknowledge your dedication and progress.

By now, you should be aware that you are in the process of creating daily habits that have the potential to transform your life.

Keep up the fantastic work, and let's continue this journey together towards personal growth and empowerment!

Start your day with three things you are grateful for in your gratitude journal.

Replace another bad habit with a good habit.

Dedicate time to learning a new skill or topic.

Challenge your mind and expand your knowledge.

Embrace the joy of lifelong learning.

Close your day by adding three things to your victory list.

If you are not willing to learn, no one can help you. If you are determined to learn, no one can stop you.

- Zig Ziglar

Day 16: Making Your Personal Commitment

Start your day with three things you are grateful for in your gratitude journal.

Replace another bad habit with a good habit.

My Personal Commitment

The concept of My Personal Commitment owes its foundation to the pioneering thoughts of Zig Ziglar, a beacon of motivation and self-improvement.

I, _____, am serious about setting and reaching my goals in my life, so on this _____day of _____, 20_____,

I promise myself that I will take the first step toward setting those goals.

I am willing to exchange temporary pleasures in the pursuit of happiness and the striving for excellence in the pursuit of my goals. I am willing to discipline my physical and emotional appetites to reach the long-range goals of happiness and accomplishment. I recognize that to reach my goals I must grow personally and have the right mental attitude, so I promise to specifically increase my knowledge in my chosen field and regularly read positive growth books and magazines. I will also attend lectures and seminars and take courses in personal growth and development.

I will utilize my time more effectively by enrolling in Automobile University and listening to motivational and educational recordings while driving or performing routine tasks at home or in the yard. I will keep a list of my activities including the completion dates for each project in my Goals Program. I further promise to list good ideas (mine and those of others) and to note thoughts, power phrases, and quotations which have meaning to me.

_____

(Sign and date)

Close your day by adding three things to your victory list.

There's a difference between interest and commitment. When you're interested in doing something, you do it only when it's convenient. When you're committed to something, you accept no excuses; only results.

\- Kenneth Blanchard

Day 17: Prioritize FaceTime Over Screen Time

Start your day with three things you are grateful for in your gratitude journal.

Replace another bad habit with a good habit.

In our modern world, technology is an integral part of our daily lives. It keeps us connected, informed, and entertained. However, it's important to use technology mindfully to maintain a healthy balance in your life.

Morning Reflection:

Start your day by setting an intention to be more mindful of your technology use. Consider the following:

Screen Time Awareness: Throughout the day, take note of how much time you spend on screens. This includes your smartphone, computer, tablet, and television. Awareness is the first step towards making positive changes.

During the Day:

As you go about your day, keep these mindful technology tips in mind:

Prioritize FaceTime: Instead of texting or emailing, consider making a phone call or, if possible, meeting someone in person. Face-to-face interactions can be more meaningful and fulfilling.

Digital Detox Evening: In the evening, try a digital detox by avoiding screen time at least two hours before bedtime. The blue light emitted by screens can interfere with your sleep quality. Use this time for relaxing activities like reading, journaling or meditating.

Evening Reflection:

Reflect on your experiences with mindful technology use today:

Challenges and Discoveries: Did you find it challenging to reduce your screen time, or did you discover that it was easier than expected?

Benefits: What benefits did you experience from prioritizing face-to-face interactions and avoiding screens in the evening? Did you feel more connected to others or sleep better?

Commitment: Commit to continuing mindful technology use in the future. Consider setting daily or weekly limits on screen time or implementing a regular digital detox evening.

Remember, the goal of this challenge is not to eliminate technology from your life but to use it in a way that enhances your overall well-being. By being mindful of your technology habits, you can strike a healthy balance between the digital world and the real world.

Close your day by adding three things to your victory list.

> *Sometimes you have to disconnect to stay connected. Remember the old days when you had eye contact during a conversation? When everyone wasn't looking down at a device in their hands? We've become so focused on that tiny screen that we forget the big picture, the people right in front of us.*
>
> - Regina Brett

Day 18: Mindful Communication

Start your day with three things you are grateful for in your gratitude journal.

Replace another bad habit with a good habit.

Today's challenge revolves around practising mindful communication. Effective communication is not just about what you say but also about how you listen and connect with others. By fostering deeper connections through conscious speaking and attentive listening, you can enhance your relationships and understanding of those around you.

Morning Preparation:

Set Your Intention: Start your day by setting a mindful communication intention. Decide that you will be present and attentive in your interactions with others.

During the Day:

Throughout the day, pay close attention to your communication habits:

Listen Actively: When engaging in conversations, make a conscious effort to listen actively. This means giving the speaker your full attention, maintaining eye contact, and refraining from formulating your response while they're still speaking.

Pause Before Responding: Before you respond to someone, take a brief pause. This allows you to gather your thoughts and respond consciously rather than reacting impulsively.

Avoid Distractions: Minimize distractions during conversations.

Put away your phone or other devices to show that you're fully present.

Practice Empathy: Try to understand the perspective and feelings of the person you're communicating with. Ask open-ended questions and express empathy when appropriate.

Evening Reflection:

Reflect on your mindful communication experiences throughout the day:

Awareness: Were you able to practice mindful communication today? Did you catch yourself being distracted or formulating responses while others were speaking?

Deeper Connections: Did you notice any positive changes in your interactions with others? Did you feel that your connections became deeper or more meaningful?

Challenges: Were there any challenges you faced in practising mindful communication? Did you find it difficult to stay present or resist distractions?

Commitment: Commit to continuing your practice of mindful communication beyond this challenge. Consider how you can integrate these habits into your daily life to strengthen your relationships.

Remember that mindful communication is a skill that can be developed over time with practice. By actively listening and speaking consciously, you not only improve your communication but also nurture more profound connections with those around you.

Close your day by adding three things to your victory list.

At this moment, there is plenty of time. In this moment, you are precisely as you should be. In this moment, there is infinite possibility.

- Victoria Moran

Day 19: The Power of Transferring Knowledge

Today's challenge is all about sharing the wisdom and knowledge you've gained during this 30-day journey with someone else. Teaching others what you've learned not only reinforces your understanding but also has a positive impact on those around you.

Morning Preparation:

Select Your Topic: Choose a specific concept or lesson from the past 18 days of the challenge that resonated with you or that you believe can benefit someone else. It could be a mindfulness technique, a goal-setting strategy, or a habit-changing exercise.

During the Day:

Throughout the day, plan and execute your knowledge-sharing session:

Identify Your Student: Find someone in your life who is willing to learn from you. It could be a family member, friend, colleague, or anyone open to receiving knowledge.

Prepare Your Lesson: Take some time to organize your thoughts and materials if necessary. Create a simple outline or presentation to structure your teaching.

Teach Mindfully: When you're ready, sit down with your chosen student and teach them what you've learned. Ensure that you explain the concept clearly and encourage them to ask questions for clarification.

Engage in Dialogue: Foster an open and engaging dialogue with your student. Encourage them to share their thoughts and insights on the topic.

Evening Reflection:

Reflect on your experience of transferring knowledge to someone else:

Impact: How did your students respond to your teaching? Did they find value in what you shared?

Clarity: Did teaching this topic to someone else enhance your understanding of it? Did you discover new insights or aspects of the concept?

Challenges: Were there any challenges in effectively conveying the knowledge? Did you face any difficulties in teaching, and how did you overcome them?

Benefits: Consider the broader benefits of sharing knowledge. How do you feel knowing that you've contributed to someone else's growth and understanding?

Commitment: Commit to continuing the practice of sharing knowledge. Think about how you can incorporate teaching and mentoring into your life moving forward.

The act of teaching is a powerful way to solidify your own knowledge and make a positive impact on others. By sharing what you've learned, you not only reinforce your own growth but also contribute to the growth of those around you.

> *The fact that I can plant a seed and it becomes a flower, share a bit of knowledge and it becomes another's, smile at someone and receive a smile in return, are to me continual spiritual exercises.*

- Leo Buscaglia

Day 20: Exercise: Revisiting the Wheel of Life

Start your day with three things you are grateful for in your gratitude journal.

Replace another bad habit with a good habit.

Today, we're going back to the foundation of this challenge, the Wheel of Life. Repeat the Wheel of Life exercise that you did on day one.

Revisiting this exercise will help you gauge your progress, set new intentions, and ensure that you're on track to create a balanced and fulfilling life.

Morning Reflection:

Review Your Previous Wheel: Begin your day by revisiting the Wheel of Life that you created on Day 1. Take a moment to remind yourself of the areas of your life that you assessed.

Self-Assessment: For each segment of the Wheel, reflect on how you've been doing over the past 20 days. Have you made improvements in certain areas? Have there been challenges or setbacks?

Set New Intentions: Based on your assessment, set new intentions for the segments of the Wheel that need attention. These could be new goals, habits, or changes you want to implement.

During the Day:

Throughout the day, focus on taking actions aligned with your new intentions:

Prioritize Your Goals: Identify one or two areas from the Wheel where you'd like to make significant progress. Make a plan for the day on how you'll work towards those goals.

Mindful Habits: As you go about your daily routines, be mindful of your intentions. Ensure that your actions align with your goals for each life segment.

Evening Reflection:

Review Your Day: Before bed, review your day's actions and decisions. Did you prioritize the areas you wanted to work on? Did you make progress in those segments?

Set Tomorrow's Intentions: Based on your reflections, set clear intentions for tomorrow. Think about how you can continue to improve and balance the various segments of your life.

Express Gratitude: Take a moment to express gratitude for the opportunities you have to work on your life balance and personal growth.

By revisiting the Wheel of Life, you're not only acknowledging your progress but also ensuring that you continue to make mindful choices in each area of your life. Remember, balance is an ongoing journey, and regular assessments and adjustments are essential for personal growth and fulfilment.

> *Balance comes in the moment when you stand up for the life you truly want for yourself, by making choices that align with that.*
>
> - Jena Coray

Day 21: Challenge: Self-Care Ritual

Today is all about you and your well-being. Self-care is a vital practice that rejuvenates your mind, body, and spirit. It's a way to show yourself love and appreciation, ultimately enhancing your overall quality of life.

Morning Mindset:

Set the Intention: As you start your day, set the intention that today is dedicated to self-care. Recognize that taking care of yourself is not selfish but necessary for your well-being.

During the Day:

Prioritize Self-Care: Identify a self-care activity that resonates with you. It could be taking a soothing bath, practising your favourite hobby, or simply setting aside time for relaxation.

Mindful Presence: While engaging in your chosen self-care activity, practice mindfulness. Be fully present in the moment, savouring the experience without distractions or worries.

Evening Reflection:

Reflect on Your Self-Care: Before bedtime, reflect on how your self-care ritual made you feel. Did it bring you peace, joy, or relaxation? Acknowledge the importance of taking time for yourself.

Gratitude for Self-Care: Express gratitude to yourself for dedicating this day to self-care. Recognize that by nurturing your well-being, you're better equipped to face life's challenges.

Remember that self-care is not an indulgence; it's a necessity for maintaining balance and resilience in your life. By prioritizing yourself today, you're investing in your overall health and happiness.

> *Even when there are a thousand things to do, cherish these unrushed moments. Make room in your heart for them. There will be many mountains to climb, but always make time to find the pastures where you can rest.*
>
> - Morgan Harper Nichols

Day 22: Challenge: Planning to Perform

Today is all about setting clear intentions and creating a plan of action to make progress in all areas of your life. It's an opportunity to align your goals with your daily actions, ensuring that you're working towards a more balanced and fulfilling life.

Morning Mindset:

Start your day with three things you are grateful for in your gratitude journal.

Set Your Intentions: As you begin your day, take a few minutes to set your intentions. Think about what you want to achieve in each area of the Wheel of Life – from your career and health to relationships and personal growth.

During the Day:

Define Your Goals: In each area of the Wheel of Life, identify specific goals you want to work towards. These goals should be clear, measurable, and achievable.

Create an Action Plan: Break down your goals into actionable steps. What can you do today to move closer to your goals in each area? Be realistic about what you can accomplish in a day.

Replace another bad habit with a good habit.

Evening Reflection:

Review Your Day: Before you go to bed, reflect on your day. Did you make progress towards your goals in each area of your life? Celebrate your achievements, no matter how small.

Adjust and Adapt: If you encounter any obstacles or challenges during the day, think about how you can overcome them moving forward. Adjust your action plan as needed.

By planning to perform and aligning your daily actions with your long-term goals, you're taking proactive steps toward creating a more balanced and fulfilling life.

> *You were born to win, but to be a winner, you must plan to win, prepare to win, and expect to win.*
>
> *If you don't have daily objectives, you qualify as a dreamer.*
>
> - Zig Ziglar

Day 23: Transformative Visualization

Today's challenge is all about harnessing the power of visualization to manifest positive change in your life. Visualization is a technique used by many successful individuals to create a mental blueprint for their desired outcomes.

Morning Mindset:

Start Your Day with Visualization: As you wake up, dedicate the first 5 minutes to visualizing that every aspect of your life is going well. Imagine a day filled with success, happiness, and accomplishments. Feel the emotions associated with this vision.

Recreate Your Self-Image: Spend another 5 minutes recreating an aspect of your self-image. This could be related to confidence, self-worth, or any trait you wish to enhance. Use seeding, visualization, and affirmations to solidify this new self-image.

During the Day:

Embody a Desired Quality: Select a quality you wish to possess, something like confidence, resilience, or patience. For 5 minutes each day, seed and visualize that you already have this quality. Feel it becoming a part of your identity. Combine seeding and visualization as one powerful technique.

Affirm Your Transformation: Throughout the day, take 5 minutes to affirm to yourself that you are already embodying this desired quality. Use positive affirmations to reinforce your belief in this transformation.

Evening Reflection:

Project of the Week: Spend 10 minutes each evening visualizing and seeding a specific goal you want to achieve this week. Use detailed visualizations, affirmations, and a strong belief in your ability to make it happen.

Visualization is a potent tool that aligns your thoughts, emotions, and actions with your goals and desires. By consistently practising these techniques, you'll strengthen your belief in your own capabilities and create a mindset that's open to positive change. Keep up the great work!

Visualizing is the art of vividly experiencing your desires within the canvas of your mind. It ignites the same sparks of reality in your brain, sending out frequencies and vibrations that resonate with your dreams. Through visualization, you wield the power to craft your life's masterpiece.

- Steyn Rossouw

Day 24: Make an Impact on the World Around You

Start your day with three things you are grateful for in your gratitude journal.

Replace another bad habit with a good habit.

Perform an intentional random act of kindness for someone. Remember to give without expectation.

It could be a small gesture or a significant favour.

Experience the joy of giving without expecting anything in return.

Performing a random act of kindness should be a daily habit. Your purpose in life is to make a difference for someone else.

Journal Your Thoughts

Spend time journaling your thoughts and emotions.

Reflect on your experiences and insights.

Gain clarity and self-awareness.

Close your day by adding three things to your victory list.

> *You cannot get through a single day without having an impact on the world around you. What you do makes a difference, and you have to decide what kind of difference you want to make.*
>
> - Jane Goodall

Day 25: Challenge: Creative Expression

Today's challenge is all about tapping into your creative side and allowing your imagination to flow freely. Creativity is a powerful tool for self-expression and problem-solving. It can also be a source of joy and inspiration.

Morning Spark:

Creative Visualization: Start your day with a creative visualization exercise. Close your eyes for 10 minutes and picture yourself in a world where anything is possible. Let your imagination run wild. Visualize scenes, scenarios, or stories that ignite your creativity and bring you joy. This exercise isn't about making sense; it's about exploring the limitless bounds of your imagination.

During the Day:

Creative Journaling: Carry a small notebook or use a note-taking app on your phone throughout the day. Whenever a creative idea, thought, or image pops into your mind, jot it down. These could be ideas for a story, a piece of art, a new recipe, or anything that excites your creative spirit.

Creative Break: Take a break during your day, preferably outdoors, and let your surroundings inspire you. Look at the world around you with fresh eyes. Notice the colours, shapes, and patterns in nature or in the urban landscape. Allow these observations to fuel your creativity.

Evening Reflection:

Creative Project: Dedicate 20-30 minutes to work on a creative project of your choice. It could be painting, drawing, writing, crafting, cooking a new recipe, or any other form of creative expression you enjoy. Let go of judgment and perfectionism; focus on the process and the joy it brings.

Creative Gratitude: Before bed, reflect on your day and express gratitude for the creative moments and ideas that emerged. Acknowledge the value of nurturing your creative side and the positive impact it had on your day.

Creativity is a wellspring of inspiration and innovation. By incorporating creative practices into your daily life, you not only enhance your problem-solving abilities but also infuse your life with more beauty and fulfilment. Enjoy your creative journey today!

Creativity is seeing what others see and thinking what no one else ever thought.

- Albert Einstein

Day 26: Challenge: Virtues Chart Exercise

Today's challenge revolves around reflecting on virtues and values that are important to you. Understanding and aligning with your core virtues can help you make more mindful decisions and lead a life in harmony with your beliefs.

Morning Contemplation:

Identify Your Core Virtues: Spend 10-15 minutes in quiet contemplation. Reflect on the virtues and values that are most meaningful to you. These could include honesty, kindness, courage, perseverance, gratitude, or any others that resonate with you. Make a list of at least five core virtues.

During the Day:

Create a Virtues Chart: Using a notebook or a digital document, create a simple chart or table with your list of core virtues. Leave enough space next to each virtue for notes or comments.

Virtue Check-In: Throughout the day, whenever you face a decision or encounter a situation that requires you to make a choice, consult your virtues chart. Consider which virtues are relevant to the decision at hand. For example, if you're dealing with a difficult colleague, you might refer to your virtues chart and see that patience and kindness are important to you.

Remember to replace one bad habit with one good habit.

Evening Reflection:

Virtue Assessment: In the evening, take a few minutes to reflect on your day. Review the decisions and choices you made, both big and small. Did you align your actions with your core virtues? Were there moments when you could have made more virtuous choices?

Virtuous Intentions: Choose one virtue from your list that you'd like to focus on tomorrow. Set an intention to embody that virtue in your thoughts, words, and actions. Write it down in your virtues chart for tomorrow.

Gratitude for Virtues: Express gratitude for the virtues that guide your life. Recognize how they contribute to your personal growth and your relationships with others. Acknowledge the positive impact they have on your daily choices.

This exercise encourages you to live intentionally and in alignment with your values. Over time, it can lead to a more fulfilling and purpose-driven life. Remember that no one is perfect, and the goal isn't to always make the "virtuous" choice but to become more aware of your values and strive to embody them in your daily life.

> *Without virtue, and without integrity, the finest talents and the most brilliant accomplishments can never gain the respect, and conciliate the esteem, of the truly valuable part of mankind.*
>
> - George Washington

Day 27: Create Your Daily Rituals for a Fulfilling Life

Today's challenge focuses on the creation of daily rituals that can help you lead a more purposeful and fulfilling life. These rituals are designed to set a positive tone for your day, guide your actions, and cultivate gratitude and mindfulness.

Morning Rituals:

Gratitude Journal: Start your day by reflecting on the things you are grateful for. Write down at least three things in your gratitude journal. This simple act can shift your focus to the positive aspects of your life and enhance your overall well-being.

Conversation with Yourself: Stand in front of a mirror and have a brief conversation with yourself. Acknowledge your worth, express self-love, and build your self-confidence. Tell yourself, "Good morning, I like you!" This self-affirmation can set a positive tone for your day.

Release Morning Worry: Spend five minutes in the morning allowing yourself to worry about anything and everything. This ritual might seem counterintuitive, but it serves as a designated time to acknowledge your worries without letting them dominate your day. Once you've expressed your concerns, mentally close the door to them and move forward with a clear mind.

Throughout the Day:

Purposeful Action: Throughout the day, remind yourself of the purpose of life, which is to help others. Be mindful of opportunities to make a positive impact on someone's life, even in small ways. Recall the story of the starfish, emphasizing that your actions, no matter how modest, can create meaningful ripples of change.

Evening Reflection:

Daily Review: Before going to sleep, take a few minutes to reflect on your day. Ask yourself if you lived your life to the fullest, made a difference in someone's life, worked towards your goals, and achieved what you set out to accomplish. This daily review helps you gain perspective on your actions and intentions.

By incorporating these rituals into your daily routine, you'll start each day with a sense of gratitude and purpose. These practices can also help you build self-esteem, manage worries effectively, and foster a mindset of kindness and contribution to others. Remember that rituals take time to become habits, so be patient and consistent as you integrate them into your daily life.

> *You'll never change your life until you change something you do daily. The secret in your success is found in your daily routine.*
>
> - John C Maxwell

Day 28: Challenge: Unplug and Reconnect with Nature

Today's challenge is all about disconnecting from the digital world and reconnecting with the natural world around you. In our fast-paced, technology-driven lives, it's essential to take a break from screens and immerse ourselves in the beauty of nature.

Morning Preparation:

Set Digital Boundaries: Before starting your day, set clear boundaries for your technology use. Decide when and where you will use your devices and when you will be unplugged. Aim to minimize screen time today.

Activities Throughout the Day:

Nature Walk: Dedicate some time to go for a nature walk. It could be in a nearby park, a forest, or even your own backyard. As you walk, pay close attention to the sights, sounds, and sensations of nature. Feel the breeze, listen to the birds, and observe the colours and textures around you.

Mindful Observation: During your nature walk, practice mindful observation. Find a spot to sit quietly, and engage your senses fully. Close your eyes, take deep breaths, and listen to the natural sounds around you. Open your eyes and take in the details of your surroundings. Notice the intricate patterns, colours, and shapes in the plants, trees, and wildlife.

Digital Detox: Challenge yourself to a digital detox for a significant part of the day. Turn off your phone or put it on silent mode. Avoid checking emails, social media, or other digital distractions. Instead, focus on being present in the moment and enjoying the world around you.

Evening Reflection:

Nature Journal: In the evening, take some time to reflect on your day in nature. Use a journal to record your thoughts, observations, and any insights you gained. Write down what you appreciated most about your outdoor experience and how it made you feel.

By spending time in nature and unplugging from screens, you can reduce stress, improve your mood, and gain a deeper appreciation for the natural world. Use this day as an opportunity to reconnect with the beauty and tranquillity of the outdoors, and consider making regular nature walks and digital detox a part of your routine for improved well-being.

Forget not that the earth delights to feel your bare feet, and the winds long to play with your hair.

- Khalil Gibran

Day 29: Challenge: Gratitude and Acts of Kindness

Today's challenge focuses on gratitude and acts of kindness. Both of these practices have the power to enhance your well-being and bring positivity into your life.

Morning Reflection:

Gratitude Journal: Begin your day by reflecting on the things you're grateful for. Write down at least three things that you appreciate in your life right now. These can be big or small, from personal achievements to simple pleasures.

Throughout the Day:

Random Acts of Kindness: Make it a mission to perform at least three random acts of kindness today. These acts can be as simple as holding the door for someone, offering a compliment, or helping a colleague with a task. The key is to perform these acts without expecting anything in return.

Express Gratitude: Whenever someone does something kind for you today, be sure to express your gratitude sincerely. A simple "thank you" can go a long way in making someone's day brighter.

Evening Reflection:

Gratitude Meditation: Before going to bed, practice a short gratitude meditation. Find a quiet and comfortable space. Close your eyes, take a few deep breaths, and focus on the things you're grateful for. Visualize these things in your mind and allow the feeling of gratitude to wash over you.

Journal Your Acts of Kindness: In your journal, make a list of the random acts of kindness you performed today and how they made you feel. Reflect on the positive impact you had on others and how it affected your own well-being.

Bonus Challenge:

If you have time and resources, consider extending your acts of kindness to the community. You could volunteer at a local charity, donate to a cause you care about, or help someone in need.

Practising gratitude and kindness not only brightens the lives of others but also brings joy and contentment into your own life. By incorporating these practices into your daily routine, you can cultivate a more positive and compassionate outlook on the world around you.

Gratitude turns what we have into enough and more. It turns denial into acceptance, chaos into order, confusion into clarity ... it makes sense of our past, brings peace for today and creates a vision for tomorrow.

- Melody Beattie

Day 30: Reflection and Celebration

Congratulations! You've reached the final day of your 30-day challenge. Today is all about reflecting on your journey, celebrating your achievements, and looking forward to what lies ahead.

Morning Reflection:

Journal Your Progress: Start your day by reviewing your journal or notes from the past 29 days. Take a moment to appreciate how far you've come and the positive changes you've experienced.

Letter to Your Future Self: Write a letter to your future self, highlighting your aspirations and intentions for the next phase of your life journey. What lessons have you learned during this challenge? What goals do you want to set for yourself going forward?

Throughout the Day:

Share Your Journey: Reach out to someone you trust and share your 30-day challenge experience. Discuss what you've learned, any breakthroughs you've had, and the impact this journey has had on your life.

Random Acts of Kindness: Continue to practice kindness by performing at least one more random act of kindness today. It's a great way to pay it forward and spread positivity.

Evening Celebration:

Celebrate Your Achievements: Treat yourself to a small

celebration or reward to acknowledge your commitment and dedication over the past month. It could be a favourite meal, a relaxing bath, or any activity that brings you joy.

Set New Goals: Take some time to set new goals and intentions for the future. What habits or practices from this challenge do you want to continue in your daily life? What new challenges or adventures do you want to pursue?

Final Journal Entry:

Reflect and Express Gratitude: In your journal, write a final entry summarizing your thoughts and feelings about this 30-day journey. Express gratitude for the experiences, lessons, and growth you've encountered along the way.

Bonus Challenge:

If you're up for it, consider sharing your 30-day challenge journey with a wider audience, whether through social media, a blog, or by inspiring others in your community to embark on their own personal growth journey.

Remember, the end of this challenge is just the beginning of a new chapter in your life. Use the momentum and insights you've gained to continue evolving, setting and achieving goals, and living a life that aligns with your values and aspirations.

Thank you for taking this journey with dedication and commitment. Your potential for growth and positive change is limitless, and every day is an opportunity to become the best version of yourself. Cheers to your continued success and personal development!

> *The more you praise and celebrate your life, the more there is in life to celebrate.*

- Oprah Winfrey

Closing Chapter: The Journey Within

As you turn the final pages of this book, I hope you've discovered the incredible power that resides within you. Throughout these chapters, we've explored the depths of self-discovery, personal growth, and transformation. You've embarked on a journey - one that has the potential to shape the rest of your life.

It's said that life is a continuous journey, and as you close this chapter, you're merely turning the page to the next adventure. You've learned that the canvas of your life is painted with the brushstrokes of your choices, actions, and beliefs. The journey within is the most profound expedition you'll ever undertake, for it leads to the very core of who you are.

In these pages, you've found tools and insights to navigate the twists and turns, the peaks and valleys of life. You've uncovered the importance of self-awareness, the magic of resilience, and the boundless potential of the human spirit.

Remember that life is not defined solely by its destinations but by the paths we choose to traverse. It's in the choices you make each day, the habits you cultivate, and the dreams you dare to pursue that your true character shines.

The challenges you've faced and the triumphs you've celebrated have sculpted you into a stronger, wiser, and more compassionate individual. Every setback has been an opportunity to learn, and every success a reminder of your limitless potential.

Never forget that your journey is unique - crafted by your experiences, shaped by your dreams, and guided by your values.

Your path may intersect with others, but your story is one-of-a-kind. Embrace it, for it is a story of growth, resilience, and transformation.

As you step away from these words and back into the world, carry with you the knowledge that the power to shape your destiny rests firmly in your hands. Embrace each new day as a chance to become a better version of yourself. Cultivate gratitude for the beauty that surrounds you and the opportunities that lie ahead.

Cherish your relationships, for they are the threads that weave the tapestry of your life. Practice kindness, not only to others but also to yourself, for self-compassion is the foundation of all growth.

And when challenges arise - and they undoubtedly will - remember that within every obstacle lies an opportunity. Embrace change, for it is the fuel of growth. Seek wisdom from your experiences, and let them be your guiding light.

In closing, know that you are the author of your story, the artist of your canvas, and the architect of your destiny. You have the power to create the life you envision - one filled with purpose, love, and fulfilment.

As you embark on the next chapter of your journey, carry these words with you: You are capable. You are resilient. You are extraordinary. The world is waiting for the unique gifts that only you can offer.

May your journey within continue to be a source of inspiration, discovery, and transformation. Your adventure has just begun, and the best is yet to come.

With heartfelt wishes for a life rich in meaning and joy,

Steyn Rossouw

In the game of life, before you get anything out, you must put something in!

- Zig Ziglar